the book of answers

littlies

the **book** of **answers**

PENGUIN BOOKS
Published by the Penguin Group
Penguin Group (NZ), 67 Apollo Drive, Rosedale,
North Shore 0632, New Zealand (a division of Pearson New Zealand Ltd)
Penguin Group (USA) Inc., 375 Hudson Street,
New York, New York 10014, USA
Penguin Group (Canada), 90 Eglinton Avenue East, Suite 700, Toronto,
Ontario, M4P 2Y3, Canada (a division of Pearson Penguin Canada Inc.)
Penguin Books Ltd, 80 Strand, London, WC2R 0RL, England
Penguin Ireland, 25 St Stephen's Green,
Dublin 2, Ireland (a division of Penguin Books Ltd)
Penguin Group (Australia), 250 Camberwell Road, Camberwell,
Victoria 3124, Australia (a division of Pearson Australia Group Pty Ltd)
Penguin Books India Pvt Ltd, 11, Community Centre,
Panchsheel Park, New Delhi – 110 017, India
Penguin Books (South Africa) (Pty) Ltd, 24 Sturdee Avenue,
Rosebank, Johannesburg 2196, South Africa

Penguin Books Ltd, Registered Offices: 80 Strand, London, WC2R 0RL, England

First published by Penguin Group (NZ), 2008
1 3 5 7 9 10 8 6 4 2

Copyright © Littlies magazine 2008

Designed by Serena Kearns, Littlies Parenting Magazine
Printed in China through Bookbuilders, Hong Kong

ISBN: 978 0143010326

A catalogue record for this book is available
from the National Library of New Zealand.

www.penguin.co.nz

The opinions expressed in The Book of Answers are those of the contributors
and not necessarily those of Littlies.

contents

contents

About The Book of Answers

Littlies Monthly Parenting Magazine is trusted by New Zealand parents of young children for the best practical parenting advice, drawing on the extensive knowledge of leading parenting experts.

What do you do when your child is the one who bites and hits? How do you cope with the shy child who stubbornly refuses to leave your side? How do you deal with temper tantrums at the supermarket or with grizzling, whining toddlers who refuse to eat? How do you stop those bed-hoppers who won't stay tucked in at night? And when, oh when, will you get a full night's sleep again?

The Book of Answers is a best-of, easy-to-read collection of *Littlies Parenting Magazine* expert answers to these and many more questions and challenges that have brought parents to the end of their parenting tether. Positive and uplifting, you'll quickly discover this book will become your all-in-one book of answers for getting through the toddler and preschool years.

Diane Levy is a well known and widely respected family therapist and parenting coach of more than 20 years experience. Presenter of the TV show,

Demons to Darlings, she is also bestselling author of three parenting titles. A sought-after speaker and one of the 2003 founding *Littlies Parenting Magazine* experts, Diane provides sound, tried-and-tested advice that parents of children under five know they can trust.

Chantal Gazal is a registered child psychologist. Her areas of expertise include parenting, child behaviour problems, ADD/ADHD and adjustment to motherhood, anxiety and depression. Author of her own book *The Happy Toddler*, Chantal joined the Littlies team of experts in 2004.

Nikki Hart is a qualified nutritionist, presenter of her own nutrition TV series *Eat Yourself Whole* and *The Fat Chance*, regular nutrition columnist and an independent nutrition consultant to many NZ companies. Nikki runs a team of nutritionists at her clinic and has been on the *Littlies* expert panel since the first issue in 2003, providing practical, commonsense nutritional advice to parents.

We would also like to thank: Dr Simon Rowley, Neonatal Paediatrician at Auckland Hospital; Dr Alex Bartle and Pinky McKay sleep experts; Dianne Krissansen, early childhood educator; Liz Donnelly, children's media specialist.

For more information about Littlies Monthly Parenting Magazine, visit

www.littlies.co.nz

hurting.

hitting & biting

I've been a parent of a child who hits other children, and I've been a parent of a child who has been hit – and I know which feels better. At least when your children are hurt you can comfort them, and feel righteous about throwing dagger glances at the offender!

When it is our own children who do the hitting, biting, scratching or shoving, we feel humiliated and inadequate. Luckily, we don't have to put up with it.

So why do they do it? The best answer I have ever come up with – whether we are thinking about our own or others' children – is, 'Because they can!' We can spend much time debating whether it is innate human behaviour or whether it's just boys being boys or girls being 'catty'. But while this may well explain how hurting others got started, it doesn't help us stop the behaviour.

prevention better than cure

Some children have a much shorter tolerance than others. You usually come to learn how long your child can play nicely and when exhaustion and frustration takes over.

Stay alert for when your child needs some 'down time'. If you can arrange it without leaving or making your child leave (maybe you can encourage

some quiet play alone near you), that is great. But if it is a case of moving them to a less stimulating environment, smile graciously, mutter, 'It's the witching hour,' and get away before the trouble escalates.

Some children seem to be born with good social skills. Other children need your guidance and support to play nicely.

Rather than using adjectives to describe behaviour – good, bad, nasty, rough – try commenting on your child's virtues or good qualities when you see them. Comment positively when you see your child showing kindness, gentleness, consideration, sharing, respect, compassion and courtesy. Catch them displaying these virtues as often as you can.

set up systems

We have a strange set of rules in many Kiwi households. 'She's your guest, so you should let her have the first turn,' followed the next day by, 'When you are at her house, it's her toys, so she's entitled to go first.' This way, our child never has entitlement!

Many 'kiddie scraps' start over the possession of a toy and escalate to hurting each other. So, have well-established rules about who has possession of things and for how long.

When a toy is being fought over, you might remove the toy for 10 minutes, 'That toy is annoying you both so much, I'll take it away for a while.' Or you might get a timer and show the

time out

I am often asked, 'How long should a child stay in time out?' The question is really, 'When is time out over?' It's over when your toddler is ready to behave appropriately. Some children show they are ready by playing calmly in their room, others by showing they have moved from anger to distress and need a quick cuddle to settle their upset feelings. Either way, if you ask 'Are you ready to behave?' you will know by the manner of the response as to whether or not time out is over.

When young children can't find words to express themselves they may resort to hitting and biting.

children how to set it for five minutes. One child has the timer, the other has the toy. When the bell goes, they swap. Although initially expect to supervise the process.

when your child has hurt

Of course, explain to your child when they have hurt someone. It is perfectly reasonable to say to a child, 'It really hurts when someone bites. How would you like that to be done to you? Now say you're sorry – really nicely! Give her a gentle hug!' This is effective when your child has hurt by mistake, though to be realistic, when this happens children are usually genuinely sorry and will spontaneously do their best to remedy the situation.

Often we are lured into thinking that explaining many times changes behaviour in unwilling children. If we find ourselves giving the same explanation for the twentieth or hundredth time – and the behaviour still isn't changing – it's time to evaluate.

Ask yourself, 'Is my child reasonably bright? Does my message typically get through

after the third or fourth explanation? Then what am I doing going over this problem again and again? Could it be that our child has no intention of changing this current behaviour?'

stopping the behaviour

The first step to stopping hitting, biting, shoving and all other unacceptable behaviours, happens in our mind. We need to decide that explaining is not powerful enough and that we are never going to tolerate our child doing these behaviours.
It also helps if we decide to be more vigilant and catch the behaviour immediately or better still, prevent it.

When you see your child hurt another, swoop over (without a word) and scoop your child to another room or place. When you get there, stand upright and say firmly, 'You know you are not allowed to hurt other children. We are going to stay here until you are ready to play nicely.' Stay there silently until your child is ready. You'll know when this occurs because the manner will change from defiance to concession. If your child is genuinely upset, a silent cuddle (without a lecture) will help settle feelings.

when your child is the hurt victim

Hopefully, the other child's parent will take action. If not, go straight over to the offending child and say very firmly, 'You know you are not allowed to do that!', and comfort your child.

By refusing to excuse or tolerate aggressive behaviour, we free our children up to be pleasant and delightful companions other children will enjoy being around. We get to watch our children interact positively and we can relax and be proud.

Diane Levy, Family Therapist

bullying

Things don't always go as planned when you're a preschooler. Life can be a school of hard knocks – the block tower collapses at the crucial moment, bedtime comes round all too quick, and there's nothing but rows of vegetables lined up for dinner – forever!

But there's one thing that no child should have to deal with and that's bullying. When it does happen to our child, as parents, we feel like rushing in and sorting it all out.

gender differences

Bullying is anything that makes a person feel intimidated and it seems gender makes a difference. Girls tend to be more subtle and indirect. Instead of snatching a toy from another child, a girl might say, 'Give me that toy or I won't be your friend anymore.' Boys are more physical and while they might push each other, they don't begrudge and are just as likely to be mates shortly after.

age differences

Older children are sometimes exposed to deliberate bullying at primary and intermediate school age, but in the preschool years, aggressiveness is generally not deliberate calculated behaviour.

Preschoolers may act aggressively to get attention,

show off, or get what they want (a toy or the next turn on the swing at the playground). They might be jealous of another child. But much of preschool behaviour is modelled from what a child has already been exposed to. So if a child snatches a toy off another child, it's likely they have had it done to them or have seen it done to someone else.

unkind words

When children begin to call other children names or use unkind words, this is the time to intervene and to teach them acceptable behaviour. Children under five aren't equipped with the maturity to effectively manage any sort of threat, including bullying, on their own – they've got enough to deal with wondering where they can hide all those veges!

react to their feelings

Children are emotional little creatures and will react according to how they're feeling at that time. Parents can help by teaching children what is appropriate and inappropriate behaviour that fits with their family values. Just as it takes children time to learn how to eat with a spoon (and they still sometimes get that wrong), it will take lots of practice for them to instinctively walk away from a situation that makes them angry or uncomfortable, and even more practice to manage that sort of situation effectively.

Using puppets, dolls, stuffed animals, or even pictures, are a great way to help illustrate appropriate responses.

Up until three and a half to four years of age, children don't have much of a concept of 'self'. So aggressive behaviour at this stage stems from something objective rather than a feeling; for example, 'I want that toy,' rather than, 'I don't like that other child and am deliberately going to do something

Older children are sometimes exposed to deliberate bullying at primary and intermediate school age, but in the pre-school years, aggressiveness is generally not deliberate calculated behaviour.

mean to him.' If there's a pattern where your child seems to pick on another child (for example, at kindy or preschool), chances are it's always about the same toy or game, not about the personality of the other child.

Similarly with children that seem to exclude other children from their games, it's likely to not be personal (maybe their elaborately thought out game only allows three people?). If your child comes home from kindy or preschool upset about this sort of incident, you might like to have a quiet word with the teacher or supervisor so they can help your child feel involved the next time.

At around four years old, a child becomes determined to do everything themselves – they are staking their claim to their place in the world. Although on the whole it's good to allow children to deal with situations on their own, if a child becomes upset or is in danger of getting hurt, parents need to take prompt action. A decisive 'NO!' is a great starting point, then remove whatever is causing the unacceptable behaviour (toy or either child) and redirect the children or explain why they cannot play in that place or that way again. If an older child is the culprit, you could suggest writing an apology card or drawing a picture.

By revisiting a situation later on at home, you will be able to teach your child other ways to deal with your feelings. Bring out the puppets (dolls, stuffed animals) again and practise what to do when you feel angry, sad, scared, and so on.

teach appropriate behaviour

The more we teach our children appropriate behaviour while they are young, the better equipped they will be to stand up to bullying, and less likely to be bullies themselves, in their school years and beyond.

if your child is the bully

If your child is being the bully, make it clear that bullying won't be tolerated and use clear consequences if it does happen. Talk about how it feels to be teased or bullied and how your child would feel if it happened to them. Also make sure your child isn't witnessing violence or aggressive behaviour between family members as this could increase aggression.

While antisocial behaviour begins early in life, without intervention it can easily snowball into a much bigger problem. By teaching our children a better way of handling their emotions and behaviour when they are young, we help them learn lifelong positive skills. And lastly, don't forget to give lots of praise for responsible behaviour.

ways to help

- Encourage friendships to help build social skills.

- Teach your child to be confident and assertive, and to react calmly using 'I' messages ('Stop that, I don't like it'), to walk away, or to find someone else to play with.

- Model the behaviour you expect from your child. Avoid making jokes that stereotype or ridicule people.

- Supervise play dates as most aggressive play happens when adults aren't looking.

- Intervene immediately when you see inappropriate behaviour. If adults are aware of bullying and don't say or do anything, children may see this as acceptance of the behaviour.

hitting at kindy

Q: I have a four and a half year old son. All in all he's a great little guy and generally a pleasure but we have a problem. At kindergarten, the teachers have been telling us that he hits other children and can be quite willful. They also say that his attention span with any given task is quite limited, that he tends to 'float' around from activity to activity without really participating much. Since this is not a problem that we encounter at home we are not sure why he is doing this at kindergarten or how to address it.

A: First of all, I would like to empathise with you and with all mothers who get greeted after kindergarten with, 'We haven't had a very good day,' and then an account of our children's misdemeanours while they have been under someone else's supervision. Your letter describes a well brought up and delightful child who recognises the boundaries set at home. At kindergarten he doesn't perceive himself as having the same boundaries and so produces behaviour that he knows better than to do at home. So the answer to your question as to why he does it is, 'Because he can!' Usually teachers try to use explaining and reasoning first and then time out as a last resort. Ideally, they should recognise that he already knows he is not allowed to hit and move him to the time out spot immediately, every time he hits. Similarly, if he declines to do as asked, he needs to be in the time out spot until he changes his mind. Alternatively, but it is second best, you could tell him very sternly that you do not want to arrive at kindergarten and hear bad stuff about his behaviour. Tell him you are going to ask every day and that you expect to hear he has been co-operative with his teachers and a good friend to his mates. If he has behaved badly, tell him you are very cross, go home in virtual silence and time out him when you get home.

Diane Levy

hitting younger brother

 Q: I would like to get some advice on my two little boys, a two year old and a two month old. I'm having lots of trouble with the older one hitting and scratching his little brother. When the new baby first came home, the oldest boy was wonderful, sometimes a bit jealous but very good in general. However, this has got worse and I'm getting a bit desperate. I've tried lots of things including time out and explaining that it hurts his brother, but nothing works.

A: It is perfectly sensible to begin by explaining that hitting hurts his little brother. If you have given the same explanation ten times and it is feeling more like 'hundreds', it isn't that he doesn't understand but that he chooses to keep doing it. I still find time out the most effective approach because we can do it as often as necessary. When parents tell me they have tried time out and it isn't working, it is usually because they are warning several times before acting or that they are only using it when they have finally had enough! If, every time he hits, you swiftly take him to time out and as you pop him in you say, 'You know you are not allowed to hurt your brother,' I am sure you will find the behaviour almost disappears within a few days.

Diane Levy

bit a friend's baby

Q: Recently my two year old bit the fingers of a friend's 13 month old baby girl. Both my Mum and my mother-in-law asked us if we bit him back after the incident. I didn't because I have heard this only encourages similar behaviour, and I really don't think I could have bit my own child anyway. But I was angry, I put him straight in the car and went home. Many of my friends' toddlers are girls and my son takes great delight in overpowering them. Now these girls are scared of him when we go visiting. He doesn't hit but smothers them until they cry. When I tell him off, he just giggles at me. My husband and I are stern with unacceptable behaviour and quick to praise good behaviour. Is it a phase or is it the beginning of bullying behaviour?

A: Let me reply to your mother and mother-in-law first. Many people tell a story that goes something like this, 'My child bit another child. I bit them straight back. They have never bitten again.' I think this works the first time because the parent responds swiftly, assertively and with such outrage, the child never repeats the behaviour and the adult believes they have discovered an excellent strategy. While it is true it can sometimes work, I can't see myself condoning or recommending it as a strategy. Don't bother with telling him off. Every time he bites or cuddles too hard, or even has that determined look which says he is about to, scoop him up (swiftly), take him (swiftly) to a different room or place, plant him there and say very, very strongly, 'You know you are not allowed to bite', or, 'You know you are not allowed to cuddle too hard.' If it is a room that suits, leave him there. If not, stay with him but don't connect with him. When you think he is ready to behave properly, he may need a quick cuddle and then he is welcome to join in again. Be prepared to repeat a swift time out as many times as needed, whether he does it five minutes later or five days later.

Diane Levy

toddler hits the new baby

Q: My toddler, aged three years, is struggling to cope with the addition of a new baby and I am at my wits' end as to how to cope with her behaviour. She has on many occasions thrown or smacked her 10-week-old sister in the head with heavy objects and toys. She will stand on the baby, pinch her, pull at her limbs, and shove her head at any given opportunity. She also hits out and throws things at me. I have tried praise and showed her how to be gentle with the baby. I've tried acknowledging her feelings by saying, 'I know it must be hard to share Mummy but it's not okay to hit the baby.' I have put her in time out and even tried removing the baby rather than her when it happens. I give her lots of quality attention and whenever possible, I make sure the baby waits rather than the other way around. But her behaviour is getting worse and I am desperate for suggestions.

A: One of the most important lessons your toddler needs to learn is that regardless of her feelings about the baby, you will never tolerate her hurting the baby and you will respond swiftly and confidently every time she even approaches the baby with menace in mind. When she does hurt the baby (or just before if you get really smart at catching her), take her to her Time Out spot or room without saying a word. When you get her to the spot or room, say very firmly, 'You know you are not allowed to hurt the baby,' and walk away. If she is still in an aggressive mood, she will need to wait there a bit longer until she changes her mind. Watch for the very first sign of aggression in the morning and make sure you are starting the day with a clear message that you will not tolerate aggression towards the baby. You may have to show her two or three times first thing, but this will help to ensure the rest of the day will be much sweeter.

Diane Levy

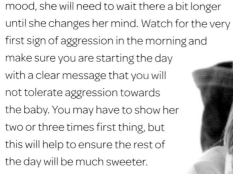

sleeping.

night time battles

'Please leave the door open and the light on. And say good night to Bear. And can I have another story?' Oh, the joys of bedtime routines! Developing good sleep habits in young children, especially once they're out of a cot and into a bed, can make the world of difference, not only for them but for sleep-deprived parents, too!

When children don't get enough sleep they're more likely to get moody and irritable and throw tantrums at the slightest aggravation. They can also develop a pattern of sleep disturbance which continues into childhood and, for some, later in life.

Sleep is important for young children; it helps growth and development, promotes learning, assists memory and concentration, and can help them to manage and control their emotions.

not enough sleep

Sleep problems affect up to 30 per cent of children and are more common if they're stressed, tired or have a temperature. Children often become over-stimulated and instead of slowing down for sleep, become hyped up and exhausted leading to sleep difficulties and tiredness. This is often identified by yawning, eye rubbing, rapid and frequent mood changes, irritability, temper tantrums and often aggressive behaviour. Developing good sleep habits includes getting to know your child's tired signs and establishing a bedtime routine for them. Children with regular bedtime routines go to sleep sooner and wake up less frequently than children with less structured bedtimes. Children need time to slide gently from the excitement of the day into the quiet of the night and, depending on how busy their day has been, winding down needs to begin at least an hour before bedtime.

sleep cycles

Young children have much shorter sleep cycles than adults. While it takes a baby longer to go from light sleep (from which they are easily aroused) to deep sleep, children reach deep sleep much more easily as they grow – which is why you can move your toddler or preschooler more easily from the car seat to bed without necessarily disturbing him.

Sleep can be divided into two distinct phases – rapid eye movement (REM) and non rapid eye movement (NREM) sleep. Both phases are extremely important for physical and mental development. NREM is particularly important for physical growth, immunity and repair, and REM is important for emotional well-being, memory storage and thought processing.

Most young children will wake a number of times during the night. Night terrors and sleep walking tend to occur in the first third of the night and children often don't remember them in the morning. Nightmares, however, occur in REM sleep near the end of sleep, often resulting in children waking from a disturbing dream and either running to Mum and Dad or sitting tight and alerting the household with a piercing wail!

sleeping methods

Our aim as parents is to obtain the benefits of good consistent

Before beginning any sleeping method, it's a good idea to check the following:

- Is your child well? Is your child safe?
- Do you have partner support?
- Are there upcoming activities or events that might interfere with the process?
- Can you cope with the stress?
- Is support from family or friends available?

Young children often have to be 'taught' to soothe themselves back to sleep. Only then will they achieve maximum benefit from their vitally important sleep – and a good night's sleep means everyone in the house is better equipped to face the new day and each other!

sleep and to help our children get back to sleep by themselves without the need to call out.

Research repeatedly reports that the quickest option to achieve this is the 'crying out' method. While this is undoubtedly the hardest on parents' emotions, it can usually be achieved within three to four nights. A child may 'cry out' for up to 2–3 hours (the older the child, the longer the persistance!), but as long as they eventually fall asleep without your presence, the next night might last only an hour, and the next 15–20 minutes. Usually by the fourth night there will be minimal crying, if any at all. Long-term evaluation of this process has failed to show any lasting psychological damage. In fact, more damage is likely to accrue if the child continues to have disrupted sleep for years on end. The 'crying out' method should not be considered, however, until a child is at least six months old.

Other methods, such as the 'Ferber' method, involve attending to your child at increasingly longer intervals until he will sleep without you. Alternatively, sit or lie close to your child until he is asleep. Then, night by night, move your bed or chair further from him. Both of these methods can take considerably longer in achieving the desired result, but they are much easier on the emotions.

If your child repeatedly gets out of bed and wakes you, the initial response should be to take him back to bed with the minimum of eye or physical contact. Positive rewards, such as a fun star chart, are excellent incentives for staying in bed.

winning bedtime battles
stay with me
Delaying tactics at bedtime – needing a drink, one more kiss, a lost toy – are a child's way of saying, 'I really want you to stay with me.' From a child's perspective, it may be difficult to relax and fall asleep if he feels stressed about being left in his room alone, especially if he can hear adults having fun in the lounge.

A consistent bedtime routine with specific rituals is important in enlisting your child's co-operation and to help her feel secure.

Consider if this is the only time of day he has your undivided attention, and if so, try to spend some special one-on-one time before bedtime so his needs aren't so intense at bedtime. If he seems especially clingy at bedtime, help by telling him the story of his day so he can process the emotional ups and downs and 'let them go'.

Around age three, you can begin setting limits at bedtime by telling him how many stories you will read before you start. To minimise delaying tactics and calling out, try to anticipate his needs. Before he gets into bed, let him get his toys in order and perhaps choose a soft toy to sleep with. Before you settle down to read, ask him, 'What is the one last thing you need to do before stories?', and sit in his room until he is sleepy.

bath time

The relaxing effects of a bath work at a physiological level as well as a psychological one. One of the triggers for sleep is a slight drop in core body temperature. A warm bath temporarily increases the core body temperature and then lowers it after a bath, making us feel drowsy. It's a good idea to take him to bed drowsy from the bath for the remainder of his bedtime routine. A few drops of lavender mixed with vegetable oil or milk or a baby bath product that incorporates the effects of aromatherapy can be added to the bath water for extra soothing effects.

magic touch

If you can get your wriggly toddler to keep still long enough to allow you to massage him, silent nights may be at your fingertips. Research has shown that children massaged daily for 15 minutes prior to bedtime fall asleep more easily. Massage reduces stress hormones, such as cortisol, and releases hormones, such as oxytocin, endorphins and melatonin, that make your child feel relaxed and drowsy. Remember to always ask your child's permission to massage him and respect his response. This way you're teaching and reinforcing to him that his body is his own and he has a right to refuse any unwanted touching. Simply stroking your child's forehead or rubbing his hands or back when he is lying in bed can also help him 'wind down' and relax.

story time

Even if you love to read several stories at bedtime, it's good to use the same story as the 'sleepy story'. The calming effects of reading together are increased if you cuddle as you read – while a story will help engage the frontal lobe of your child's brain, and this will inhibit motor impulses, body contact during cuddles will encourage your child to release sleep inducing hormones. Dim lighting from a bedside lamp (rather than a bright overhead light) can help stimulate melatonin, the sleep inducing hormone.

food for sleep

Restless sleep can be related to sensitivity to additives in processed foods and soft drinks which can hype up behaviour and prevent your child from sleeping well. Some sensitive children may be affected by naturally occurring chemicals, such as salicylates in otherwise healthy foods like grapes, oranges, strawberries and tomatoes. Try reducing the amount or

combination of foods, so instead of giving him grapes and strawberries for dessert after a meal of spaghetti with tomato sauce, keep to the mantra 'all things in moderation' and try these foods separately in smaller amounts. Bedtime snacks can also affect sleep. For instance, high protein foods can trigger the production of dopamine, a hormone that will keep your child aroused, whereas a banana will help boost the levels of tryptophan, the substance needed to make the mood-stabilising (calming) chemical serotonin which encourages sound sleep.

early risers

Typically children are ready to wake at the first ray of sunshine. Blackout blinds or heavy, dark-coloured curtains to block out light could help. Also put a lidded cup of water and a few safe toys or books within reach next to the bed so he can quietly amuse himself to hopefully buy you extra sleep time. If it seems early morning noise from outside or from other family members could be waking him, set a clock radio on a station playing either classical music or in between stations so it plays white noise. Set it to start playing before your child normally wakes, so that helps him to sleep through the early morning sounds. If he goes to bed early and has a good sleep but wakes early, he's probably waking because he's had enough sleep. Try gradually adjusting his bedtime at night (move later by around 10–15 minutes every few nights). Otherwise just 'wear it' and have an early morning cuddle in bed with him or get up and have some fun as you greet the day together.

**Dr Alex Bartle and
Pinky McKay,
Sleep Experts**

daytime sleeps

The age children drop day sleeps varies greatly. If your child is staying up later at night or is wide awake at naptime, it's probably time to drop the nap. At first you will need to keep her busy and try to avoid car rides in the late afternoon so she doesn't fall asleep at 4 p.m. then bounce back again after dinner. If she is at daycare where naps are a specific time, it's best to conform to this routine and enjoy some quiet play at night rather than battle over bedtime because she isn't tired. Discuss her readiness for dropping her nap, and ways to manage this smoothly, with her daycare. For a while she'll likely need an occasional 'catch-up' sleep which you could encourage on weekends when late nights don't matter as much.

from cot to bed

For some children moving from cot to bed is another exciting step to being a 'big kid' and they make the transition with ease. But for other little ones, 'the big bed' can be more than a little daunting. So when is the best time to make the move and how can you make it easy for your child?

Most children are ready somewhere between two and three years old, but really it depends on when your child feels ready. It's best to avoid doing it at the same time as other important changes such as moving house, starting a new kindy or daycare, or the arrival of a new sibling.

If you are expecting another baby, it's better to move your child into a bed at least a month or two before your due date so there is not a feeling of being pushed out of the cot. It will also give them a chance to settle into the new bed before baby's arrival. But if your child is already climbing out of the cot, making the move into a bed sooner rather than later is a safer option.

There's plenty of choice when it comes to 'first beds'. You might like to consider a cot-bed or a toddler bed to bridge the gap between a cot and a bed. However, these will only be suitable for a couple of years before the need to upgrade to a full-size bed – young children grow quickly! Or

you may feel your child can cope with a full-sized single bed from the very beginning. Bunk beds are popular and exciting for young children, especially as they pre-empt small friends visiting for sleepovers, although it is recommended children under six do not sleep in the top bunk.

If you're buying a second-hand bed or using a 'hand-me-down' bed, it's a good idea to buy a new mattress. Older mattresses may not conform to current safety standards and it may be full of dust mites (the average person sheds a pound of skin a year which dust mites feed on).

If possible, push one side of the bed against the wall and make sure there is no gap between the wall and the mattress as your child could get stuck if they roll over. Bed rails or guards can help stop falls or alternatively put something soft on the floor – the old cot mattress, a soft rug or a duvet.

If the bed is near a window check your child can't

climb out of it, or put a safety lock on the window. Check the bedroom is safe from any toys or furniture that could hurt them if they tumble out of bed, or fall when climbing out of bed to play instead of sleeping!

Once you have decided to move your child from the cot, it's a good idea to warn in advance of what's to come. Make it appealing and involve your child in setting up the new bed if you can.

When you feel your child is ready to move from cot to the bed, talk about the change a few days beforehand to ease the transition.

easing the transition

- If possible, get your child to help choose the new bed, the sheets and bed covers or a new soft toy.
- Make the bed a fun place to be – cuddle up and read books together and point out pictures of people sleeping in a bed like a 'big person'.

- If you have the space, put the bed in the same room as the cot well before the transition so they get used to the idea of a bed being in their room. You could even let your child use the bed for daytime naps and the cot at night for awhile.

- Play games together and put some dolls and teddies in the bed.

- When you're finally ready for the transition, put the bed in the same place as the cot used to stand.

- Be prepared for your child to initially wake a few times while getting used to the bed. A bed is also easier to climb out of on the way into yours – be consistent and return the culprit to bed each time!

- To help keep your child settled through the night put fluorescent stars or shapes on the walls or use a night light. Alternatively keep the door ajar with a soft light in the hallway on.

If your child still doesn't take to having a big bed, it may simply be too early. Revert back to using a cot for a while and wait until your child seems ready again. The good news is that no matter how long your child takes, they all get there in the end!

night time waking

Q: My two year old has just started sleeping in a bed. While he has adapted well to the change and is usually easy to put down, there is the odd night he'll try his luck at getting up again! The bigger problem for us is his night waking. With the exception of one or two nights, he appears regularly at the side of my bed anytime between 11 p.m. and 4 a.m. Generally he's easy to settle back into his own bed, but night after night of broken sleep is starting to take its toll on us. Consequently I've been taking the 'easy' option and letting him get into bed with me. He sleeps well when he does this but I am worried he may become a permanent feature if I continue to let him. We have had a lot of change recently – a long overseas holiday followed by a long stay at his grandparents and then moving into a new home. I'm not sure if this has anything to do with his night waking as he's always been a good sleeper with two hours sleep during the day.

A: Many children who have been good sleepers change their sleeping patterns when they make the transition from a cot to a bed. This can also be the case if there have been a lot of changes in the family. While your son was in his cot it wouldn't have occurred to him to get out, or rather he wasn't able to get out, and so the 'boundary' of the cot gave him no option and a certain security. Now in a bed, he perceives himself as having the option of visiting rights. When he comes out to visit, scoop him up – rather like a robot – and pop him back into bed. Don't settle him because he needs to learn how to settle himself when he surfaces during the night. If this hasn't convinced him (in about three nights or 10 'returns'), close the door after you return him as most children will prefer to stay in bed so they can have the door open and feel connected to the family.

Diane Levy

night time fear

Q: I have a son nearly three years old. He was a good sleeper – happy to go to his room and sleep in the dark. However, he has developed a fear of the dark, and needs me to wait until he is asleep. If I leave before he's asleep he cries and gets out of bed to come and find me. He wakes up frequently and runs crying into our bedroom, looking over his shoulder as if he is being chased. When I take him back, I have to wait until he is asleep before I can leave but he seems to wake within a few hours and the process is repeated. I'm pregnant and am finding repeatedly taking him back tiring. Sometimes I just let him sleep in bed with us, which I know is not good, and my husband and I also have a poor night's sleep.

A: Many of our children, who have previously been good sleepers, somehow lose the ability and need our help and support to get it back. Often it is as a result of some fright or an illness when they have needed us, and sometimes it happens for no particular reason that we can point to, our children appear traumatised and lose their confidence in their ability to get off to sleep on their own. If your son has trouble getting off to sleep on his own at bedtime, it is likely that he won't be able to get back to sleep on his own when he wakes in the middle of the night, so it is important to fix the going-to-sleep-at-bedtime issue first. Tuck him in with a couple of toys and a book and leave the light on. Make an excuse to pop away (e.g. I am going to put the kettle on) and get back within about 30 seconds. Tell him he's wonderful and that you will pop back as soon and get back within a minute. Keep extending your time away a minute at a time and eventually you will go in to find he has drifted happily off to sleep. Once he is going off to sleep easily on his own at bedtime, you can begin walking him back to his bed (without a word is the most powerful way) when he appears at your bedside in the middle of the night. Another suggestion: make a 'Bravery Kit' from a shoebox, a small torch, a soft toy and a 'weapon'. (Small plastic daggers fit in a Bravery Kit and are excellent for keeping dragons away!) At bedtime, when you are tucking him in, say, 'Let's check your Bravery Kit.' Here's your torch so you can check your room. Here's your Fluffy dog to keep you company. And here's your dagger to protect you.' Put the Bravery Kit next to him, kiss him goodnight and go. Leave the light on if he prefers to go to sleep with it on. When he appears by your bedside, go back to his bed and check the Bravery Kit again. Kiss him good night and go back to bed confident that he has all that he needs to go off to sleep. Since most children choose to fall asleep with their torch still on, keep a supply of batteries!

Diane Levy

not sleeping at daycare

Q: We have a sleep problem with a 20 month girl who has been attending our daycare for a year. At home she sleeps for Mum but doesn't seem to want to sleep for us. We have tried to place her on a mattress for six months. We lie beside her and try to pacify her, even though she seems to be very angry with us. But we give up after 15 minutes as many feel that is long enough. Some are now questioning whether we can try for a little longer. She has shown signs of settling just as the time expires.

A: It is difficult when a child has one parenting culture at home and a different one at daycare. However, most children easily adapt to different behaviours in different places. When I first started counselling, I was taught, 'Start where the client is at and lead them to a better place.' I know it is a pain, but I would recommend you go back to the position where the child is relaxed and trusting. Start from there and then move on gradually. Have whoever is in charge of the sleeping room – or you may even need to assign a second person for a couple of weeks – take the little girl onto her lap and let her go to sleep there. If the carer waits for 10 minutes after the child is fully asleep (so that the child has gone into a deeper phase of sleep), they will be able to move her gently onto a sleeping mat. If she wakes upset have the carer put her back on her lap until she goes back to sleep or is fully awake and ready to play. Once this becomes simple to achieve, keep it up for at least another week until the child fully trusts that she can relax and go off to sleep at daycare. Once that is fully established, let the child lie on the mat next to the adult's lap – possibly with a back rub – so that she can learn to go off to sleep that way. Next sit close without a back rub. After that, I am sure the child will be able to sleep on the mat unassisted. The trick is to allow the child to trust (that she will be supported) at each step before moving on to the next.

Diane Levy

tucking her in over and over again

Q: I have an 11 month old who has been escaping from under the blankets for about 2–3 months. This has increased dramatically over the last week. Yesterday I tucked her in ten times when it was naptime and she just got out again to play. Then last night, she escaped three times during the night and called for us to tuck her back in again. This is a game that I am losing patience with very rapidly.

A: When we are used to tucking our babies in, walking out of the room and they lie there and drift off to sleep, it comes as a rude shock when they discover other ideas. About this time, it is useful to realise that one human being simply cannot make another one go to sleep. We can make them stay in their cot (until they climb out). We can make them stay in their bed (until they climb out). We can make them stay in their room but we cannot make them go to sleep. If it is during the day, I suggest that you decide you are entitled to an hour's break. If it is in the evening, I suggest you decide that you have been a lovely mother all day and now you are not particularly interested until tomorrow morning. Dress your child warmly as if she is going to sleep all night on top of her covers. That way, you don't have to worry about her being out of her blankets. Make the decision that, once you have tucked her in and kissed her good night, your mothering job is finished for awhile unless there is an emergency. She may well sit up and play but when she is tired, she will lie down and drift off to sleep. Once she is asleep, go in and rearrange her and tuck her in.

Diane Levy

early morning risers

Q: We have a three and a half year old girl and a two year old boy, both in beds and separate rooms, and both wake between 5–5.30 a.m. every morning. They are normally in bed before 7.30 p.m. with the same bedtime routine. If our daughter has a sleep during the day, she goes to bed about 8 p.m. Our boy has huge day sleeps (two to three hours) to catch up on his early morning. I have tried for a week waking him during his day sleep after one and a half hours – he goes to bed more easily at night, but it hasn't altered his wake-up time. My husband and I take turns getting up early with the kids, but not until 6 a.m. We try not to give them any breakfast until about 6.30 a.m. We have tried treating it like a night time wake – no talking, straight back to bed. Is it time to be cutting out those day sleeps?

A: Early morning wakers are hard to shift. Sometimes, all we can do is continue to have early morning wakers but not let them be early morning risers! In other words, they can wake as early as they like, but they are not coming out of their rooms until you are ready. Shortening the daytime sleep usually results in a very grumpy child if you wake them before they are ready to wake naturally. The most useful way of getting them to sleep later – or at least staying in their rooms later without a fuss – is to get there in small steps. If it's still dark at 5–5.30 a.m., use a night light or torch or allow them to put on their light. Whenever they wake, they can always find a few toys to play with and hop back into bed to keep warm and play quietly. Decide for yourself what time you are prepared to get up – say 5.45 a.m., quarter of an hour later than they normally do – and at that time let them get up and come out of their rooms. A video may get you another half-hour's peace. It is not worth nagging, growling and cajoling. They are either allowed up or they are not. Once they can manage to wait it out until 5.45 a.m., decide that you are not getting up to them until 6 a.m. Keep stretching it by quarter of an hour to the time you want. You cannot make a child sleep but you can make them stay in their room. Often, when using this method, the child works out that when they wake early, there is an awfully long time to getting up time and they roll over and go back to sleep.

Diane Levy

screams the house down

Q: I have a 3 year old who, through my own fault I guess, will not sleep through the night in her own bed. I have tried many times to establish a routine, pyjamas, a story and cuddle and leaving her to cry in her own bed, popping in at extended intervals. She will scream the house down – sometimes even making herself sick! I have always sat beside her bed and she has always played with my hair until she falls asleep. I feel like I'm looking for a secret solution but I guess I'm looking for advice on how to not give in and to persevere, without feeling like an ogre.

A: It is definitely not too late to make changes. I recommend doing things in a way that is not traumatic for you or for your daughter – even though that means it will take some time. Firstly, your daughter needs to be able to go off to sleep on her own at bedtime so that when she wakes in the middle of the night, she will be capable of going back to sleep on her own. For the present when she wakes at night, just let her into your bed and get the best night's sleep you can. At bedtime, your first job is to guard your own boundaries. Nobody – not even your beloved daughter – should treat your body in ways you don't want. Pull up a comfortable armchair right next to her bed, take a good book and tell her you are willing to sit with her until she goes off to sleep. No talking. No hair touching. Or you will leave the room for five minutes and then be willing to try again. Once this works easily – be prepared for about ten days – move your chair to the middle of the room. Once this works easily, move your chair to the doorway. You may or may not have to do one more week with your chair just outside the doorway.

Diane Levy

takes two hours to settle

Q: Our 21 month old daughter is a terrible sleeper. She gets up anywhere between one and six times every night, and after 19 months we're finding it a long time to cope without a solid sleep. While she's had quite an unsettling time in the past few months, life is back to normal now. The battle starts at bedtime. She doesn't want to go to bed, wants me to stay with her or wants to get into our bed. We've tried leaving her to settle on her own but this can take two hours or longer. It seems the only thing left for us to do is to shut the door on her, but I'm not a great fan of this. Once asleep, she will last to around 12.30 a.m. or, if we're lucky, 3 a.m! She comes into our bedroom and wants to get into bed with us. It can take us five attempts to get her back to her bed, then we shut the door, which is usually followed by screaming (sometimes for up to three hours!). Some people said we should leave her to scream. Are we doing the right thing, or are there other methods to make our life easier – her excessive sobbing breaks my heart?

A: I don't agree with the people who have told you to leave her to scream. You say she has had quite an unsettling time in the past few months but things are now back to normal. While things may be back to normal in terms of household routines, it may not be back to normal for her and quite possibly she doesn't have the confidence you won't vanish from her again. I imagine her fears get worse at bedtime and during the night. It's likely she's quite clingy during the day and gets distressed if she can't find you. When you leave a room, tell her and offer her the opportunity to come with you or to keep on playing. The simplest way to reassure her that you are there at night is to let her sleep with you. If you don't want to do that – or after you've done it for a couple of weeks – put a comfy chair near her bed and at bedtime, take yourself a good book, settle down and say, 'Mummy's here. You're safe', and read until she goes to sleep. When she calls out during the night, wrap yourself in a warm duvet and sit on the chair, 'Mummy's here. You're safe', and doze until she falls asleep. After a week or two when she is feeling confident to go off to sleep with you right next to her, you can move your chair to the middle of the room for a few days, and then to the doorway for a few days following that. After that, use the pop-in method to support her to stay in her room without you being there.

Diane Levy

never been a good sleeper

Q: After four years, I have had enough and need some advice on what to do with my four year old boy. He has never been a good sleeper, waking at least three times a night with either bad dreams or just to come into our bed. He is now at preschool four mornings a week which I thought would make him more tired so he'd have a better sleep. If anything he is worse and by the end of the week he is not worth knowing. He has a regular bed time of 7–7.30 p.m., and we have cut down sugar intake during the day. He is not toilet trained at night and we thought perhaps his bladder was waking him. We tried waking him and taking him to the toilet, but he sleeps very deeply and is hard to wake.

A: Keep him in night nappies, sort the sleep out first and then you will be in a much better position to deal with the toilet training. All of us surface several times a night and mostly we just roll over and go back to sleep. If you want him to do this, you have to be sure that he knows how to go off to sleep on his own. Similarly, all of us have nightmares from which we surface, feel very grateful that we are in our own bed and generally go back to sleep. Make sure that he goes to bed before he is so tired that he just 'flakes out'. He needs to go to bed sufficiently alert so that he spends at least 15 minutes quietly leafing through a book or playing with a few 'quiet' toys and then take himself off to sleep. Once you are confident that he is capable of taking himself off to sleep at bedtime, you will feel a lot more confident that he can repeat that process in the middle of the night. When he shows up next to your bed, remember it is your job to return him to bed but not to help him go to sleep. Don't try to cajole, comfort or explain. Get up without a word, walk him back to his bed, tuck him in and say, 'You are fine, darling. See you in the morning,' and go back to your bed.

Diane Levy

won't stay in bed

Q: We have a 26 month old son who has gone from being a great sleeper to a complete nightmare. He moved out of her cot and into a bed (at his request). We felt we did all the right things beforehand; put the bed in his room for a few weeks before he actually started to sleep in it, read stories sitting on it, got dressed on it, had fun on it, etc. Initially he was okay sleeping in it, but now he takes two hours to settle. We have tried all sorts of things to get him to stay in bed – going in every few minutes, talking to him, ignoring him and just putting him back to bed, taking his favourite toy away, staying in the room – but none of this has worked. He normally gets out of bed to play. Daytime sleeps are not an issue – he sleeps for a maximum of two hours so he is tired when it's bedtime.

A: The simplest would be to put him back in his cot so he can't get down and play. If that isn't an option, try the 'pop-in' method again but add a slight variation. At bedtime, tell him you will pop in to see how nicely he is lying in his bed. (It is fine for him to have a few bed toys to play with until he drifts off to sleep.) Leave the door open. Pop in after 30 seconds and tell him how wonderful he is and that you will come back to see how good he is being, staying in his bed. Return in a minute and, once again, tell him how wonderful he is staying in her bed and that you will come back in a couple of minutes. Then go in after two minutes, three minutes, four minutes, and so on, each time telling him how wonderful he is staying in bed. If you go in and find him out of his bed, or if he comes out, tell him that because he got out of bed, the door will be closed for five minutes. After that, leave the door open and resume 'popping in' to find out how good he is being. I know it's time consuming, but it would be most effective to start again at 30 seconds if you can. If you have had three lots of door-closing in one evening, you are being 'had'. Tell him you will see him in the morning and close the door until he is asleep. If you suspect he has hopped out of bed, approach somewhat heavy-footed so he can hear you coming and has the chance to scuttle back to bed and be lying there 'with an innocent face' when you come in!

Diane Levy

connect.

mum, dad are you listening?

Effective communication with your child involves two important components – namely listening and talking. Children who feel listened to are far more likely and willing to listen to their parents – which is a good thing!

Positive listening and talking skills of your own will show children respect, love and understanding, and the manner in which you communicate plays a significant role in shaping the people your children will become. This all affects their behaviour and personality, how they communicate and relate to you and others, and the way they feel about themselves and the world.

effective listening

really be present
Stop whatever you are doing and really pay attention to what your child is saying. Show you are listening with your body language. Go down to your child's level and look in their eyes.

Really listen to what is being said. Look at the facial and body language as this will often communicate the feeling of what's being said.

your child says	reflective listening	ineffective listening
'I hate Tim. He just took away my ball again!'	'You're angry at Tim for taking away your ball.'	'Don't talk like that. You don't hate Tim. You love him.'
'I'm really scared to go to the doctor.'	'You're scared that the doctor may hurt you.'	'You'll be fine. There's nothing to be upset about.'
'Everyone is ignoring me.'	'You would like us to give you more attention.'	'What are you talking about? Everyone gives you attention.'
'I wish Olivia was never born!'	'You're feeling a little left out since your sister was born.'	'That's ridiculous. I know how much affection you feel towards your sister.'
'I don't want to go to kindy today.'	'You'd rather stay home with Mummy today.'	'Oh that's not true. You have so much fun at kindy!'
'I can't stand Jack. He always disturbs me when I'm playing.'	'You're upset with Jack for disturbing your play.'	'Take it easy. Jack is not that bad.'

acknowledge what they have said

Show you are listening by smiling, saying, 'I see', or nodding your head if you agree . Ask questions if you need to clarify anything. You may also want to use your child's name, 'Is that right Sam?' It is a wonderful way to connect with your child and to let him know you are really present.

don't interrupt

Even if what your child is saying isn't of interest to you or you disagree with it, allow him to have his say and then respond. If you find he is going on for too long, wait for a pause in their conversation and try diverting attention to something else.

also try reflective listening

This is one of the most important skills you can teach your child in order to open the lines of communication now and into the teens. It requires that you observe and listen to your child and then reflect back what has been said to you. Reflective listening is particularly helpful to use when your child has strong feelings or a problem.

The key to really being present with your child is to understand his perspective rather than yours. As the old saying goes put yourself in his shoes.

Repeat to your child what you heard him say. Once you have listened and tried to understand

his experience, reflect his feelings back to him as you interpreted them: 'You seem angry with Carol'; 'You don't want me to leave.' Even if you don't agree with the way your child is feeling, don't try changing his feelings. Denying a person's feelings does not change a person. If you acknowledge your child's feelings, he is far more likely to speak to you honestly because he feels you respect and understand him.

Avoid lecturing or rescuing your child. If your child has a problem that needs resolving, ask and see if he can come up with his own solution first. Only if he fails to come up with anything suitable, do you then suggest some of your own.

Children are far better off if they learn to make decisions and solve problems on their own from a young age. It helps them to develop independence, confidence and self-control. The table on page 45 shows ways you can use good listening in everyday situations.

Reflective listening is especially useful in helping your child to understand his own feelings and to communicate with words. When you describe for him what he is experiencing, you help him learn the words so he can more easily express his own feelings in future.

When you reflect your child's negative feelings, it can help to calm him down and to become less intense because of the satisfaction your child feels from just being heard and understood.

listening helps in other ways

- Parents can acknowledge children's requests without giving in, 'I understand that you really want that toy but I can't buy it for you.'

- It helps to make children's feelings more bearable.

- It teaches children to solve problems.

- It builds children's self-esteem.

- It opens up the lines of communication and helps parents to develop a trusting and loving relationship with their child.

- Children feel heard and understood.

- Children are more likely to behave.

Listening attentively to your child helps him to feel special, important and loved and valued – and these are the best ingredients for nurturing a happy and confident child!

Chantal Gazal, Registered Psychologist

The key to really being present with your child is to understand his perspective rather than yours. As the old saying goes put yourself in his shoes.

talking effectively & respectfully

Talking effectively and respectfully with your children, especially when disciplining, will have plentiful positive results.

How you talk to and listen to your children makes them who they are. Talking effectively and re-spectfully helps children to feel happy, secure and confident, as well as teaching them how to express themselves with confidence, to forge friendships and to be assertive throughout their growing years. But perhaps most importantly, they will later be more willing to communicate with you when they have concerns about the many issues they will face through their early school and teenage years.

go down to their level

Go down to their level, ask them to look into your eyes and say, 'Do you have your listening ears on?' Use a firm and serious tone of voice. You may also want to use a certain cue (a tap on their shoulders) that indicates to them it's time to listen to you. Remove any distractions that may interfere with your conversation.

Remember that your child's attention span is short. Say one or two simple sentences. Go

straight to making your point and briefly explain the consequences if there are any.

if you are getting angry

Try as much as possible to keep your frustration under control. If you use a calm matter-of-fact voice, even when you're angry, children will view your dialogue as a conversation rather than a confrontation and will therefore be more likely to listen to you attentively. In turn, they will also learn to communicate calmly when they are angry.

Ask them to repeat what you've said just to make sure they have heard you. If they are obviously listening to you or clearly repeat what you have said, let them know you've noticed, 'Excellent listening, James', or, 'I like it when you pay attention to what I say, Natasha.'

Focus on outlining their inappropriate behaviour rather than attacking them. After all, it's the behaviour you are disciplining.

'I' versus 'you' messages	
'I'm really upset the room is such a mess.'	'You are so messy.'
'I don't like it when you ignore me.'	'You are naughty ignoring me when I talk to you.'
'Please get down. I'm tired. I need a rest before playing with you.'	'You're so annoying jumping all over me like that.'
'I feel so angry when you speak to me like that.'	'What's wrong with you, talking to me like that?'
'I get really frustrated when you forget to close the door yet again.'	'What are you doing, leaving the door open again!'

avoid lecturing

Once you have had a chance to express yourself, allow your children their say. Avoid lecturing them. If you can, wait until you are both calm and have the time to be fully focused on the conversation. Speak to your children the way you would like them to speak to you. Remember they will learn how to communicate to you and others mostly from the way you communicate to them.

Aim to spend lots of time asking your children how they are doing, praising them, noticing their good behaviour and giving them a smile or cuddle. Don't just use their names when you're correcting them. Say your child's name often to make conversation with your child more personal and meaningful. Children are sensitive beings and easily take negative statements to heart. Try to avoid using negative tone-of-voice or negative communication strategies. Instead, here are some ways you can speak more effectively to your children, especially when disciplining them.

avoid negative labels

They are damaging to a child's self-esteem. Children take labels to heart and often feel hurt and shameful. Believing the label, children live up to it and act accordingly – lazy, stupid, mean, etc.
example: 'Stop crying like a baby.'
better alternative: Focus on the behaviour, 'I can't help you until you use your words and tell me what's bothering you.'

avoid inducing fear

Children become frightened rather than learning appropriate desirable behaviours. If used often, the parent-child bond is affected.
example: 'Do as I say or you're getting a smack.'
better alternative: Use a consequence to teach the behaviour you want, 'I need you to pack-up

Children tend to respond better to 'I' messages as these don't judge, blame or criticise in the same way as 'You' messages do.

with me right now, please, otherwise it's time out.'

avoid comparison

This encourages resentment rather than compliance.
example: 'Why can't you be more like your sister?'
better alternative: Focus on the behaviour, 'I need you to turn off the television and come to the table.' Issue a consequence if necessary, 'If you don't do as you're told, there will be no playing with the blocks again after dinner.'

avoid foul language

Children learn most from watching their parents.
example: 'You're driving me bloody crazy!'
better alternative: Use an 'I' message, 'I get so frustrated when I call your name and you ignore me.'

avoid using 'always' or 'never'

It gives your child the message they have permanent undesirable traits, making them feel unacceptable and hurting self-esteem.
example: 'You never do as I ask.'
better alternative: Stick to the issue and issue a consequence if necessary, 'I need you to come here right now otherwise I will put away the doll you're playing with.'

Talking and communicating effectively with your child lays the building blocks for an open, honest, positive and loving relationship for years to come.

Chantal Gazal, Registered Psychologist

but . . . why?

'If she asks why one more time, I think I am going to scream!'
Somewhere between the ages of four and five, we may well find
ourselves thinking the same thing.

A child's happy curiosity is one of life's special gifts that, if handled patiently and with a sparkle in your eye, can develop your own imagination and open your own mind to the many wonders around us.

It means your child has the ability and vocabulary to formulate questions, to use adverbs and to understand there is cause and effect. It means you have a child who has curiosity and is searching for insight. Most 'Why?' questions will be about your child trying to understand the world he finds himself in. He deserves thoughtful and respectful responses.

why, why and why?

You may wish you had paid more attention in school science classes – Why is the sky blue? Why can't we fly? You will need to do some fancy footwork – Why is Uncle Fred allowed to burp when you say I'm rude? Why are you allowed to say that word – when I am not? And you will need to think through your schedule – Why can't we go to the park to play today?

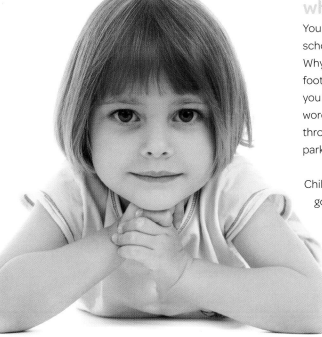

Children also seem to love keeping the sequence going. Why are leaves green? Because they have special stuff called chlorophyll which makes them green. But why do they have clor-ro-fil? So they can trap the sun's energy. But why do they need energy? See what I mean about science classes!

53

why is it why after why?

There are two reasons why children respond to your carefully thought-out reply with another Why? They most likely have a genuine desire to find out more and in this case it requires us to reply respectfully and as accurately as we can. Try getting out age-appropriate books from your local library on subjects that interest your child.

The second reason is they have discovered it is a way of keeping parents engaged. Let's face it! Our children have a fairly limited ability for keeping us engaged in conversation. They don't have the capacity to ask us what we think about the latest political situation or how we should contribute to a natural disaster on the other side of the world. If they wish to keep us engaged and they are only four years old, continuously asking why is a sure-fire way of keeping conversation going.

Sometimes recognising this as it is happening can arm you with the patience to deal with it. You might choose to keep going with the question and answer session. You might show your child something else of interest. You might choose to play a game or read a book together. You might invite his help with whatever task you were doing so you can keep a conversation going as you work together.

can't stand it

If you can't find the capacity to keep answering the constant questioning, try not to denigrate your child. Tempting though it is, it is unkind to berate your child with comments such as, 'Why do you always have to keep asking questions?'

He is just following a developmental imperative. Instead tell it like it is. 'Mummy is tired and just doesn't have the energy for any more talking right now. Would a cuddle help?' Wrap your arms around him and don't say another word (even if he asks, 'Why are you tired, Mummy?' Aargh!), until he wanders off to do something more interesting.

embarrassing why's

We've likely all been there. We are minding our own business at the supermarket and hear our child ask (in a loud, clear voice), 'Mummy, why does that man walk funny?' We pretend our child isn't really ours but it's not that convincing when he is sitting in our trolley. If we ignore him, he will just have to ask louder and possibly even point out the poor

person to be sure we understand him better. There is nothing I know that teaches children on-the-spot NOT to ask why about something they find greatly interesting. I do, however, know that a private discussion along the lines of being kind, appropriate and tactful may save you and your child's embarrassment on future occasions.

talk about it

If your child is old enough to be asking why, he is old enough to learn some other concepts. When you get home talk about the incident. Talk about what it is like for people who are overweight, elderly, or with unusual features to have others commenting or staring. Most children are kind and don't like to deliberately hurt others. Explain that while they were correct and the man walked differently, it was unkind to say so out loud because it would be hurtful to that person's feelings.

need to know basis

Our children still need to let us know when they have seen something they wish to tell us about. I found it useful to set up a hand signal so our children could let me know if they had seen something of interest but knew it wouldn't be appreciated if they commented. Instead of verbally telling me, they would squeeze my hand and I would silently (with a squeeze back) acknowledge I had also seen it.

When we got back to the car, I would firstly recognise their achievement of keeping quiet so we did not hurt other's feelings, and then talk about whatever it was that had been seen. Of course we all know the first question was always: 'WHY?'

Diane Levy, Family Therapist

If you can't find the capacity to keep answering the constant questioning, try not to denigrate your child. Most 'Why?' questions will be about your child trying to understand the world he finds himself in. He deserves thoughtful and respectful responses.

social skills.

making friends

I often get phone calls from parents worrying about their child's ability to make and keep friends and to join in.

The first question I usually ask is, 'What is your child's style? Are they outgoing or reserved? Do they join in right away or do they prefer to watch for awhile before joining in?'

of child we have, it is important we acknowledge the worthiness of that style. The outgoing child rarely needs our support in social situations; they just take off and play.

our social child

The gregarious, social child joins in quickly and easily. They seem to have an inborn ability to join the group and happily do whatever everyone else is doing. We rarely even think about their social skills. At the other end of the spectrum is the child who likes to sit by us and watch and wait until they fully understand what is going on, before they tentatively sidle up and join in. Both extremes (and most styles in between) are all natural ways of behaving. Whichever style

our shy child

With reserved children, the temptation is to encourage them to join in before they are ready. We tend to find ourselves cajoling a reluctant child to leave our side or explaining within earshot to another adult, that he or she is a bit shy.

We should avoid speaking about our children as if they are not there and we should certainly avoid landing them with labels such as 'shy'. The best way to give our children the courage to join in play with others is to allow them to stay with us – an arm around their shoulder while letting them observe until they are ready to go and look more closely, and allowing them to return if they need to.

Our skill in supporting mildly anxious feelings without rescuing or lecturing makes our children feel warmly accepted by us. In return they will naturally expect to be warmly accepted by friends.

our bossy child

Extremes of bossiness are not useful social skills. The bossy child may try to control all social situations to their liking and change the rules of the game to ensure they win or get their own way. They may even decide who can and can't join in!

Although this behaviour may work to their advantage at the beginning, sooner or later children will start moving away to find more pleasant company. The best way we can help our bossy child to be more socially graceful out of the home, is to teach them clear rules of play inside the home.

Set up the rules of the game before you start. Work out transparently fair systems around who goes first and how long the turn will be. Adults playing board games with children can help a great deal in modelling how to take turns, good-natured winning and gracious acceptance of defeat. When we have an only child, it is very easy to let him or her go first and to win every time – this, however, is not serving our child well when amongst peers.

our helpless child

When our children's response to things that are not going their way is to cry, sulk or simply 'turn helpless', we run the risk that other children will find someone who is more fun to play with. Again, we can do a lot at home to make sure we do not reward helpless behaviour.

Some children keep friends for a lifetime. Others have a new 'best friend' every 20 minutes. Some fall in and out of friendships, while some children pick up friends wherever they go. As with most learning, our children grow and develop through experimenting and practice.

If we have a child who easily gives up, it is easy to fall into the habit of lecturing about the disadvantages of giving up or of cajoling and making concessions so he or she will keep going. It is of far greater use to your child to call a break for 10 minutes and then offer a chance to try again. This keeps the responsibility with the child for being a good sport and enjoying the game.

If they still don't want to join in, let them know they are welcome to watch or to be in the same room. Keep the game going for a while so they know that just because they opted out, the good times can keep going without them.

good friends don't hit

When a child is having trouble with friendships, we can ask ourselves, 'Is my child a good friend?' Good friends don't hit, bite or pinch each other, or snatch toys and push others out of the way.

If you know that some of these unacceptable behaviours are part of the reason your child doesn't have friends, don't excuse it with, 'But she's just trying to join in and doesn't know how.' Even if you haven't got the identical behaviour at home, you will usually have a behaviour that is similar. For example, your child doesn't hit at home, but will snatch a toy off a younger sibling and swap with them another one to keep the sibling quiet.

Develop a 'No tolerance' policy for unacceptable behaviours at home and you will be amazed how fast your child transfers the same restraint into the playground.

you're not my friend

Some children keep friends for a lifetime. Others have a new 'best friend' every 20 minutes. Some fall in and out of friendships, while some children pick up friends wherever they go. As with most learning, our children grow and develop through experimenting and practice.

It is easy for us to feel happy with all possible variations, until our child is hurt by a 'friend' not allowing your child to join in the game because, 'You're not my friend anymore.'

What should a parent do about your own upset child? A good cuddle while you mutter, 'That's horrible for you', usually enables your child to feel comforted and to decide whether to try again or to play with someone more welcoming.

It is important we don't allow unkindness or a culture of exclusion. Approach the group and say, 'You've just been very

unkind saying Kate is not your friend. Find a way of including everyone.' Then closely observe to make sure that it happens.

skills for playing

Make sure your children have the skills to play the sorts of games their friends like to play. Give them lots of opportunities to master playground equipment so when they are with their friends, they can focus on playing with them while on the jungle-gym or slides.

Ensure your child can ride a trike if little friends are going to be riding around at

the park together. Make sure your child knows the sort of board games, construction toys and 'dolly adventures' that friends are likely to want to be doing when they visit their place.

enough friends

By making sure your children have the skills required to be a good friend, you will usually ensure that they have 'enough' friends. How many is enough?

We need to be careful not to impose our friendship quota when deciding whether our children are making friends or not. Some children have everybody as their best friends. Some children favour one or two best friends. Others don't have anyone they particularly favour, while some like to play alongside other children without necessarily being highly interactive.

As long as our children know how to play and how not to be antisocial, the odds are their social development will keep progressing nicely.

Our job as parents is to monitor their behaviour, to understand their style and to set up opportunities for them to spend time with their peers. Their job is to have the fun and enjoy the benefits of social play!

**Diane Levy,
Family Therapist**

separation anxiety

We've all had that heart-rending experience. We need to leave. Our child doesn't want us to leave. We explain all the benefits of staying. We elaborate on all the wonderful opportunities there will be once we are out of sight. We are convinced. Our child isn't!

We peel them off like an octopus. We make a dash for the door. We depart to the sound of piercing wails. Long after we have driven away, we can still hear them echoing in our ears.

We fret and worry until pick-up time, imagining our precious child upset and suffering.
'How did it go?' we tentatively ask.
'Oh! He was just fine. The moment you were out of sight, he settled down and had a wonderful time.'

The next time, our child starts as dawn is breaking.
'Mummy, am I going to kindergarten today?'
'Yes, darling. You will have such a wonderful time there with so many wonderful things to do.'
'Mummy, I don't want to go. Please, don't make me go.'

some do; some don't

All children are designed to be attached to their mother, to seek her out and to feel comforted and safe when they are in her arms. They are surrounded by many other people fairly constantly in their lives and they learn that they can trust other people to look after them.

Some children are of the 'go to anyone' variety and others object if you make eye contact with them before they have had a chance to 'suss you out'.

As parents we are very tough on ourselves. We somehow believe that it is a mark of parental competence to have children who can part easily from us and manage well without us. Conversely, if we have a child who finds it hard to let us go, we somehow feel as if we have failed a parenting test. I think we are being far too tough on ourselves.

The reality is that some children find it easy to be self-reliant and easily say goodbye and enjoy a new experience without us. Other children find this more difficult. It is more a matter of our child's style and temperament than of upbringing.

your child's pace

Provided we do it at our child's pace, all children can learn that people other than their immediate family can be trusted to care for them.

When babies first begin to crawl, they will go a few feet away from us, get busy for a while and then scuttle back when they feel the need for security or comfort. Soon, they feel able to go into the next room, but when it gets scary, they rush back to find us again for some comfort.

As they get older they are able to manage without us for increasingly longer intervals as they go to daycare, kindy, primary school, high school and eventually overseas!

managing without us

What makes our children able to manage without us is threefold.

As parents we are very tough on ourselves. We somehow believe that it is a mark of parental competence to have children who can part easily from us and manage well without us.

It is their ability to hold us in their hearts and minds so that they know we will return.

Firstly, it is their ability to hold us in their hearts and minds so that they know we will return.

Secondly, their experience teaches them that we can go away and yet will return within an interval of time that they can manage.

Thirdly, we replace ourselves with another trusted adult. Dad, grandparents, aunties and uncles, babysitters, crèche caregivers, kindy teachers can all become people whom our child can trust to keep them safe, understand their wants and meet their needs.

leaving easily

For most children, we go through a simple routine when we drop them at kindy. We walk in with them, we greet their teacher, and they participate in hanging up their jacket and in hanging up their bag. We help them find their first activity.

When they are well settled in, we say goodbye and leave. They may look up and farewell us or they may be so engrossed in whatever they are doing that they barely notice or bother to farewell us. We go off happy and secure in the knowledge that our children can manage without us.

my child gets really upset

Some children absolutely dread the moment of our departure. We walk in with them clinging and wailing and they refuse to look at the teacher – let alone greet them. They passively let us hang up their bag and their jacket. They refuse to settle to any activity and reject our suggestions for what might be interesting.

What is going on here? These children simply do no want us to leave. The dialogue going on in their heads is something like,

do something

These children require a different approach. We take them in, we hang up their gear and, at this moment, there is no point in prolonging their agony. Ask your child, 'Who would you like to cuddle you while Mummy leaves?'

Say to the chosen caregiver, 'Can Jamie stay with you while I go?' If necessary, peel him off, hand him over, kiss him goodbye and leave swiftly without a backward glance.

he may still be upset

Your child may still be dreadfully upset. You may still have to depart with his cries ringing in your ears. But, you have left him safely in someone's arms.

That person will comfort him and settle him into an activity. The main difference is he knows that the caregiver is there for the whole day and that he can rush to her anytime he needs care or comfort. He will rapidly settle and be ready to join in the fun.

you can be like everyone

Soon your child will race away from you at the gate, scarcely remembering to say, 'Goodbye'. When you arrive to pick him up, he may even scream, 'Go away. I'm busy. I don't want to come home.'

Then you can be like the rest of us who cringe with embarrassment when we ponder what sort of home we run that our children don't even wish to come home!

Diane Levy, Family Therapist

'So if I settle down to play, Mum will leave. So, I can't possibly settle down to play because that will make Mum leave.'

In trying to settle them in, we place them in an impossible conflict with themselves – and us!

teaching children to say thank you

By the time our children are around three years old, we would like them to have moved from 'demand, demand, demand', through 'automatic manners' to showing signs of gratitude for the good things that happen to them in life.

However, if we wish them to get there, we are going to have to train them. So where do we start if we want our children to feel gratitude and to think about what they are grateful for? The best place to start is to teach them the actions of gratitude. Once the actions are automatic, the feelings and comprehension usually follow.

model the actions and words of gratitude

As soon as your child can comprehend speech (or starting from today as you read this article!), model the actions and words of gratitude.

When your baby lies still enough to be changed, say, 'Thank you for lying so still.' When your toddler gives you something you requested, tell him, 'Good boy. Thank you. What a big help you are!'

Most of us would have been taught that we should use 'praise' to shape the behaviours we want How much nicer would it be, to be genuinely appreciative and show gratitude to our little ones so they see the virtue of gratitude in their daily lives and naturally learn to copy that behaviour.

teach manners

If you teach your children the action part of gratitude, the rest usually follows. Ask your high-chaired toddler to hand you his plate, 'Give your plate to Mummy, please.' When he gives it to you, respond with, 'Thank you for giving Mummy your plate.' When he asks you for a cracker, model, 'Can I have a cracker please Mummy?' Even if he is only capable of a 'Peeeese', he has done well and deserves your gratitude. If you insist on 'please' and 'thank you' every time, it should soon become automatic.

insist on manners

When you insist your child thanks his host before he leaves a birthday party or a play date, he may be doing it initially as a matter of social form without genuine meaning, but if it becomes a habit, the gratitude will follow.

When you pick up your child from kindy or childcare, or when you leave Nana's always thank them and get your child to say thank you too. When your child is given a gift or when grandparents arrive with a treat, insist your child says thank you and don't permit the handover to be completed until good manners are shown (remember gratitude may take awhile).

bedtime chats

You can help promote gratitude by lying with your child at bed-time, and help him talk about all good things that happened that day and all the people who made them happen. You may be amazed how long your child can make gratitude last as they think up one more thing to be grateful for, just to keep you in their bed!

If you are parenting in a two-parent family, be sure your child knows that purchases come from both parents. 'We must remember to thank Dad when he gets home.' 'Show Mum what we bought for you today.' By thanking the other parent, it helps your child learn to be grateful for the role both parents play in the family.

I have a treasured memory of my late father-in-law who, in the 28 years he was in my life, never left a meal table without saying to his wife, 'Thank you, Darling.' What a model of gratitude for his son, his grandchildren and anyone who joined them for a meal.

Diane Levy, Family Therapist

If you insist on 'please' and 'thank you' every time, it should soon become automatic.

shyness

Shyness may range from the child who watches cautiously from the sideline, to the child who buries a head against our leg and refuses to be coaxed out, to the 'fake shyness' of the child who yells, 'I can't do that! I'm much too shy.'

why are children shy?

As with most patterns of child behaviour, shyness is partly the temperament children are born with and partly the way children are raised. If we ourselves are or were shy, we are inclined to worry that we have somehow transmitted this to our children.

Some children seem to have always had a natural reserve. They are initially cautious with new people and in new situations. They like to watch rather than leap in. They are hesitant to try new things. They prefer to play with one or two familiar friends rather than take part in games involving crowds.

While I do believe that we should always respect a child's natural personality, I also believe that there are ordinary courtesies that we should expect from our children at home and when they are out. For cheerful, outgoing children, this usually comes naturally and easily. For our more reserved children, we need to be responsible for teaching them good manners and social skills.

While respecting our children's personalities, if we think that our children have learned shyness, we can help them to 'unlearn' the excuse of shyness, so that they do not become hampered with the label of 'He's very shy, you know. I used to be, too.'

won't he just grow out of it?

While it is true that many children do become less shy as they grow older, they miss out on a lot of fun and many opportunities while waiting for this to happen. If we think shyness is hampering the fun to be had at gatherings, I think it is worth taking steps early on to help our children interact positively with adults and with other children.

teach them good manners

All of our children benefit from being able to say 'please' and 'thank you' in an audible voice, from being able to look people in the eye (if this is culturally appropriate) and greet them courteously and to be able to go and say, 'Thank you for having me,' as they leave someone's house.

By insisting on good manners from our shy children as well as our outgoing children, we set up an expectation of capability. Since our children will usually meet our expectations, our demanding a minimum standard of courtesy stands them in good stead. Generally people like well-mannered children.

If we start at home with 'please' and 'thank you' and insist that our children greet any visitors to our home, we set them up to be competent outside the home where they may be feeling more shy.

supporting our shy child

It is important that we support our child rather than excuse

Not every child is going to be an outgoing little person who just loves to be the centre of attention and thrives on crowds and noise. Neither would we want all our children to be like that.

While it is true that many children do become less shy as they grow older, they miss out on a lot of fun and many opportunities while waiting for this to happen.

them. If we know that our child finds it hard to greet or thank unfamiliar adults, we can make sure that we are there to support them. It is often a good idea to lift small children so that they are at eye-level, or to put an arm around them as they get the words of greeting out. That way, they have our support without our leaping to rescue them.

Reserved but co-operative children often find it helpful if we 'cue' the expected behaviour. 'When Mrs Jones answers the door, I want you to say: "Hello Mrs Jones, nice to see you." I'll be right next to you.'

when shyness is rude

Sometimes our children are smart enough to disguise rudeness as shyness and often we fall into the trap of believing them. If your child can speak loudly and clearly when he is in a demanding mood, he is quite capable of meeting and greeting people who come to your home. If your child is quite capable of greeting grandma and grandpa enthusiastically when they arrive at his house with a present, he is equally capable of greeting them politely and warmly when he goes to their house.

If your child is happily settled at kindy or crèche and is familiar with his teachers, I would recommend that he begin each morning by greeting his teachers by name if they are at the door when he arrives.

kind can be unhelpful

Picture the scene. Your child is generally capable of 'meeting and greeting' when it suits him. You have reminded him in the car of what you expect. You walk up to the door and you greet the welcoming adult. You put an arm around your child and say, 'Say hello to Mrs Jones.' Your child buries his head in your jeans and refuses to look up. You ask one more time. And then Mrs Jones, meaning to be kind and helpful to you both, says, 'Oh! That's alright! He's probably feeling a bit shy.'

Not helpful, Mrs Jones! I know you meant to be kind and put Mum – and possibly the child – out of their agony. But you have inadvertently undermined the mother and reinforced in the child's mind that his shyness makes him incapable and incompetent.

helping children join in

Sometimes we find ourselves in a situation where we have outgoing children, but the visiting child is somewhat more reserved. Give a shy child the chance to settle in and assess his surroundings. Let him stay with his mother or father for a while even if all the others are racing around outside. If the child has been left to play at your house, he may well feel safer initially, staying with you – an adult – until he feels settled in.

After a 'settling in' period, offer to take him outside and help him join in. Take him by the hand or put an arm around him. Go over to the children who are playing and assign a child to look after him. 'Jenny, James is ready to join in now. Would you please start him off and make sure he gets his turn.'

That way you have supported him to join the group, given him a 'minder' to ensure fair play and by using the words 'he is ready now', you have implied that he is perfectly capable but just took a little while to warm up.

not everyone is a party animal

Not every child is going to be an outgoing little person who just loves to be the centre of attention and thrives on crowds and noise. Neither would we want all our children to be like that.

By respecting our children's innate personality as the starting point, by insisting on courtesy, by teaching our children social skills, by supporting our more reserved children as they learn to overcome their feelings of shyness and behave appropriately, we do them a favour.

Diane Levy, Family Therapist

interrupting

When our babies are small, their needs are so urgent we interrupt what we are doing to attend to them. While they are this little, we can carry on with our adult lives and still meet their needs.

When our toddlers become more interactive, their interruptions are cute and compelling. It is such a delight that our toddler enjoys books enough to rush over with a certain page for us to read or look at that we happily drop what we are doing.

cute turns into demand

Then it starts to get annoying. We used to be able to meet our toddler's needs with a phone held by our shoulder. Now we have a toddler with a loud voice dragging us to show us what he wants.

We answer the phone and two shrieking children decide to play 'chasee' around our legs. We are trying to have a chat with a friend and our kindy child simply has to recite – right now – every nursery rhyme in her extremely long repertoire. We sit down and catch up with our partner about the day and our feisty four year old squirms into the middle and announces, 'No, Mummy! I'm telling Daddy about my day!'

normal but not necessary

It is well within the range of normal behaviour for our children to interrupt us. However, just because it is normal doesn't make it necessary. Even if we have inadvertently been part of our children learning to interrupt, it doesn't

mean they can't unlearn interruption behaviour and learn instead to wait patiently – or even impatiently – for their turn.

support waiting behaviour

When your child comes up to you and wants to say something, put an arm around him and say, 'Just wait until Mummy finishes her sentence.' Finish your sentence and then say, 'Good boy for waiting. What was it you wanted to tell me?' Gradually, lengthen the amount of time your child is kept waiting – always with an arm around him to show that you know he's there and that you appreciate his restraint.

friendly reminders

A friendly but firm reminder about expected behaviour will have two effects. Firstly, it makes clear the boundaries of acceptable behaviour and secondly, if we are clear about our expectations, our children will often rise to meet them. When your child interrupts, say strongly, 'You know you're not allowed to interrupt when someone else is speaking. Please wait until I have finished.'

It's a lovely idea to teach our children to say, 'Excuse me,' if they need to interrupt. However, we've all fallen into the trap of our children extending this to full permission to interrupt, whenever they choose as long as they preceed with, 'Excuse me, please.'

Particularly if you are dealing with a strong-willed child, it is a good idea to set your boundary and give your child some control in the situation. 'I just need to finish the dishes and then I will come and see what you are building. Do you want to wait with me or should I come to you when I am finished?'

with visitors

You are entitled to have a quiet cup of coffee with a friend or a chat with your partner. Begin by setting up expectations. 'Lucy

It is well within the range of normal behaviour for our children to interrupt us.

Even if you can drop what you are doing right away, it is a good idea to value your own time as well as your child's request. 'I'd be happy to read to you after morning tea. Just now I need to do my work. You are welcome to bring your blocks in here and be with me while I make the bed. Or you could help Mummy instead.

is coming around soon, so let's choose some toys for you to play with while the grown-ups talk.' Allow your child centre stage at the beginning, and then let him know he is welcome to be around you provided he is quiet, or he can play in his room and you will call him to join you for afternoon tea. If you get repeated interruptions, commit yourself to action. Scoop your child up, take him to another room and explain very firmly that he is not to interrupt.

on the phone

Have two or three special toys by the phone saved only for phone calls. This is a great idea but only if your child is willing to go along with it! Otherwise, when your child gets up to bad behaviour while you are on the phone, excuse yourself, scoop him into his room, and say, 'I'll be back as soon as the call is finished.' Finish the call (relatively quickly) and then open the door saying, 'I've finished now,' and walk away without further comment. If your child is upset, a cuddle is perfectly appropriate.

time out

If all these kind and encouraging processes are not effective, it is useful to remember that there is a household rule – No Interrupting. Take your child to time out and say, 'You know you're not allowed to interrupt. I'll pop back to see if you are ready to join us without interrupting.' Be prepared to repeat this and if you have a few episodes in a row, lengthen the time before you go back in.

Although, superficially, we are teaching our children not to interrupt, we are actually teaching them valuable life skills: to be able to tolerate a small frustration; to be able to briefly delay gratification; and to be obedient to small courtesies and rules. And who knows, we may even get to finish the odd conversation or cup of coffee!

Diane Levy, Family Therapist

toilet talk

'I have never been able to give a satisfactory reply to questions such as, "Why does my child have to use naughty words?", "How come my child, who is usually difficult to understand, can pronounce swear words with startling clarity?" And my favourite question, "Where do they get those words from?!"'

Parents tend to believe such words must be learned at kindy or day care since they don't use 'undesirable' words at home. Teachers tend to believe they must have been learned at home as such words are not permitted at kindy or day care. So to start with, accept that we may never know who they learned it from, why the attraction to a particular word, or how they learned it so quickly. Then it will be easier to move on to what we are going to do about it.

don't ask

One of the problems when my children came home with a new – of course they didn't learn it at home! - rude word is that they always caught me by surprise. Just as I thought we were having a conversation in civilised English, one would blurt out with some Anglo-Saxon classic. In my stunned (or appalled) state and before I could stop myself, I would say "What did you say?" Of course then my child felt obliged to repeat it! If, at this point, you bale your child up and complain vigorously about

the language they have just used, they can cheer-fully respond with, "But you asked!"

what does it mean?

Many of us have naively tried the "If you knew what it meant, you wouldn't use it" approach. I have given children accurate information about what certain words mean and every now and again they have been sufficiently shocked not to use it again within my earshot.

However, I need to point out that my two older children are now in their thirties and my youngest is 20 so the words I was explaining to them when they were youngsters may not be words children use in 2006. I suspect the problem with this approach is likely to be two-fold.

Firstly the range and style of words acceptable in pop songs and on TV is becoming ruder and ruder. Secondly, as I race through my contemporary list of 'rude' vocabulary in my head, I cannot think of any words I would be prepared to explain to my children today.

So we are better off not getting too literal and just assuming it's the thought that counts rather than the precise meaning.

just ignore it

The most commonly-given advice is to ignore it. When they discover it doesn't get them attention, the words will lose their attraction. While this sounds plausible, I have never been able to get it to work.

Let's face it, the fact words are rude or a bit naughty is what makes them attractive, so it is very unlikely our children will give them up lightly.

The part of 'just ignore it' I recommend is to simply not go making a big fuss about the words. The more you are appalled, horrified, mortified, upset or amused and entertained, the more your child will repeat them.

amused or appalled?

It not only depends on the words used, but on where they are used. If your child is playing in her room or on the swing on her own and happily crooning away, 'Poo-poo, stink, bum,' and possibly laughing in delight at her own wit, I'd be inclined to stay deaf and invisible.

If, however, she is yelling at the top of her voice for the entire neighbourhood to hear, or she is preceding it with 'Mummy's a...', I would take a very different attitude. And certainly if she uses the words as weapons to hurl at you when she doesn't agree with a decision you have made, such as, 'You're a mean stinky-poo bum bum Mummy', I would take a very different attitude too.

wash your mouth out

In our parent's or grandparent's day, using naughty words frequently resulted in having your mouth washed out with soap, mustard on the tongue, fines or spankings.

I don't think any of these are suitable today. But if you want to make the point your child needs to have control over her mouth and that the words used have unpleasant or rude connotations, you may like to insist your child stops what she is doing and goes and cleans her teeth. The good bit about this is it inconveniences the child, ties and replaces the grubby talk nicely with a clean and wholesome activity, and makes it clear you won't tolerate the use of those words within earshot of a grown-up.

Some people, however, may not want to tie teeth cleaning as a consequence with teeth cleaning as a desirable activity.

make up your mind

The first step is to be clear in your own mind which words and situations you will let go and which ones you find completely unacceptable. Once you are clear which words you will not allow in your household, you will need to act every time you hear those words being used.

Every time you hear the rude word or words, scoop your child outside or to a spot in your house and say strongly and clearly, 'You know we don't use those words in our house. I'll be back to ask you if you're ready to control the words that come out of your mouth.' Go back and check, 'Do you have your words under your control?'

I was just saying 'bumper'

Some children get really smart and change a few letters of a word just so they can stay out of trouble. It goes back to their intention. If they have thought out a new and acceptable word to express annoyance or because they like the alliteration, I would let it go. But if they are just being smart and trying to outwit you, feel free to add their new, creative word to the list of unacceptables.

Before you start bouncing on your child's inappropriate language, have a careful listen to the language in your own home. We are on very shaky ground when we reprimand our child for the use of a particular word, only to have the child rejoin, 'But Daddy uses it all the time!'

Diane Levy, Family Therapist

Don't make a big fuss about the words. The more you are appalled, horrified, mortified, upset or amused and entertained, the more your child will repeat them.

separation stress

Q: I work part-time and my son goes to daycare. It's a small, homely daycare with consistent teachers. My son has been going for over a year now and parting is still a difficult, traumatic experience. As soon as I have put away his things, he buries himself in my chest and holds on tightly. I usually talk to the teacher for a few minutes and then peel him off me, but he inevitably cries hysterically, wriggles and reaches out for me. I say goodbye and leave. Not once have I gone back to him. Wouldn't you think that after a year of this, three times a week, he would have learned that crying doesn't make me stay? The teachers are fantastic with him and one of them will always give him a handover cuddle. They are very skilled at settling children (this was mentioned in their ERO report). The teachers say he is happy and when he is picked up (usually by my husband) he is playing happily. My son is very sensitive and he is disturbed by loud, sudden noises and has been this way since birth. He loves to go out shopping, to playgrounds, the beach but not other people's houses, especially if there are other young children. He usually clings for around 30 minutes before settling to play and will only leave my side for a few minutes at a time. Classes like Jumping Beans are hopeless as I can't peel him off me or if I do, he waves goodbye to everything and heads for the door to leave!

A: I am so sorry that you and your son have to endure an upset every time you leave him. Some children seem to be able to say goodbye easily and get on with all the exciting activities that daycare has to offer and others continue to find separation awful. You seem to be taking all the right steps and nothing is changing. Since he does settle after you have gone, I think the best interpretation of his behaviour is that he finds the moment of separation from you (rather than being away from you which he seems to handle without upset) very difficult and a rapid handover is the least painful option. The fact that he loves to go shopping, to playgrounds and to the beach, shows that you are raising a child who is happy to have new adventures but derives enormous confidence from having you there. In social situations which he finds difficult, continue to allow him to stay with you until he feels safe, to make forays out and return to you as often as he needs. You are doing the right thing. I don't agree that leaving him more often will make him more confident and ready to part from you. Keep going at the pace that suits him.

Diane Levy

shy or controlling

Q: My four-year-old daughter is often bright, cheerful and eager to please, but she is also an extremely determined child who will exert enormous effort in order to stay in control of a situation. Today I was driven to distraction at our kindy outing. She wanted to ride her bike to the park but I explained to her that we were all walking and her bike needed to stay at kindy. From then on, she was unhappy and walked slowly. Then she complained that she needed a drink (which unfortunately I had forgotten), so she began pushing and kicking me angrily for having forgotten it. I went into a cafe and got her a cup of water, but she didn't really drink it. As a result, we arrived late at the park and she refused to go close or join in with the other children, telling me she felt too scared and didn't want to be the girl who arrived late. For the next hour I darted between my two-year-old, who was having a great time on the swings, and her. She had moved further away, crying loudly and curled into a ball causing much concern among the other parents if I was away from her. I offered to take her home, but she said she would, "Never move and never leave this park!" I know only too well what it's like trying to get her to walk anywhere when she doesn't feel like it, so I was left isolated from the group, feeling helpless and unable to do anything with her. Eventually we had to make a large scene because I felt there was no point staying any longer. She angrily tried to push the pram over with her little brother in it but after some soothing words, agreed to squash into the pram with him and be pushed home. I haven't followed up with any punishment because I don't know if she was just feeling shy and it was annoying me, or was it her obstinate attempt to control me? I don't want her growing up completely unable to follow along with a group at appropriate times. Help!

A: First of all, my heartfelt sympathies! I have been that mother whose child is refusing to join fun activities, who is deliberately sabotaging every effort to give her a good time, and who is making a totally unreasonable and very public fuss while all the other children are having a good time. When your little girl is being bright, cheerful and eager to please, enjoy every moment. When she is in a contrary mood, forget about appeasement. When our children get into a determinedly unreasonable frame of mind, they see our attempts at explaining, reasonable compromise or persuasion, as weakness. The harder we try, the harder they push – so we might as well put in our boundaries right from the start, let them make their great fuss at the beginning and let them discover we are not here to be treated badly by them. It is easy to view things with hindsight, but here is another way you may have handled it. Your little girl was having 'one of those days'. She needed you to say, 'I know you would rather ride (acknowledge her feelings) but everyone is walking today (put in the boundary).' Walk slightly ahead of her pace and don't engage in discussion while she is being unpleasant (keep that boundary going.) 'I'm sorry you are thirsty. When we get to the park, I will ask one of the other mums if we can have some water.' (No further discussion about it, keep that boundary going.) At the park, your daughter has options. She can join in the fun or she can stay curled in a crying ball. Let either choice be acceptable to you. In the meantime, you go and have a good time with the other mums, popping back occasionally to offer your upset child a cuddle and to see if she is ready to join you. (Remember, you can only give support to a child who is willing to receive it.) Rather than hauling her away from the fun – with all the fuss and aggravation that goes with it – stay and show her she has choices and you are not going to be involved with, or intimidated by, her totally unnecessary miserable behaviour.

Diane Levy

don't want to be your friend

Q: We have an almost four year old daughter who goes to morning kindy. On quite a few occasions, I have overheard her saying to her peers that she doesn't want to be their friend any more, in a nasty sarcastic manner. I have been told this is typical behaviour of her age and she will eventually grow out of it. She plays closely with one other girl, who tends to be the one my daughter says this to. I have seen this child quite upset from her comments. My daughter has even come home from kindy and started saying it to her younger sister (but she doesn't fully understand what it means). We have tried explaining it is not okay to say this, as it hurts her friend's feelings and they may not want to play with her if she keeps telling them she doesn't want to be their friend. We understand she should be able to use her voice if she doesn't want to play with someone, but what is the appropriate thing to encourage her to say? Will she just grow out of it?

A: I know that people intend to be kind and reassuring when they say things such as, 'She'll eventually grow out of it', but these are of little help especially as they leave us with the false idea that: 1. There isn't much we *should* do about it, and 2. There isn't much we *can* do about it. Rather than tackle the words or behaviour, you will find it much more effective to tackle the virtue. You want to encourage the virtue of kindness and forbid the 'lack of virtue' of unkindness. Fortunately, your daughter is showing the same traits towards her sister, so you have the opportunity to change your four year old's behaviour at home and trust that it will generalise to kindy. Every time you hear her being unkind, go over to her and say, 'You know we don't treat people unkindly. Now let me hear a kind response to your sister.' If she cannot come up with one right away, pop her into her room and tell her that she can come out as soon as she is ready to be kind. When you do hear her speaking kindly and inclusively, be sure to comment favourably on it.

Diane Levy

easily quits

Q: I have an adorable and bright four year old who attends a preschool and kindy. She has no problems with me leaving her there and happily joins in at mat time. At preschool they have aerobics, which took her many months of watching before she joined in, but now she loves it. She also asked to do ballet this year, but after the first visit, decided she didn't like it. Part of this may have been to do with the fact the parents had to leave the room and return at the end of class. I'm worried that she will end up being a quitter, trying things once and then giving up. The same happened with soccer and drama with her trying them once and quitting. It makes us angry, which we know isn't helping, but it's really hard when the other children do what they are expected and have fun, while our daughter is having tantrums on the sidelines. We want to expose her to different things but wonder if we are starting her too young. What's the best approach to help her through this? We don't want to damage her self-esteem at such a young age.

A: A clue seems to lie in your statement, 'It took her many months of watching aerobics but then she joined in and now she loves it.' Your daughter sounds as if she is the type of child who may only enjoy doing things after she has watched for long enough to know exactly what to do and until she has confidence in the teacher. Presumably she is hesitant to try new things and needs your support to do so. If so, it's no wonder she dislikes being part of a class where parents are asked to leave the room and return later. This is not the right learning atmosphere for her at this age and stage – with the exception of preschool and kindy where she goes often enough and long enough to build up a relationship with her teachers and caregivers. At age four, it is well within the realms of perfectly normal for a child not to like being left on her own with a group of children, unfamiliar activities and a classroom teacher. (It is also well within the realms of perfectly normal for those children who are confident enough to readily join in straight away and without a parent present.) It is largely a matter of a child's temperament and that is something we don't get to choose. By all means, give her lots of experiences where she can watch and learn and eventually join in with the confidence and safety of knowing you are there. Wait until after her first year of school when she really understands about following directions from a teacher without Mum there. By then she will have much more confidence and be ready to benefit from the sort of wonderful opportunities you want her to have.

Diane Levy

don't go mum

Q: My three year old cries every time I leave him at kindy. Initially he started going once a week but recently we increased this to three times a week. He just doesn't settle, so this term I have stayed with him for the first couple of sessions to help settle him. But when it's time for me to go, he hangs on to my legs and cries until he's red in the face. I've tried every strategy (except consistency!), from explaining that I'm going and will be 'back soon', to waiting until he's involved in an activity and then either saying a brisk goodbye or sneaking off. Staff are really supportive, walking with me to the gate and trying to distract him, but they have lots of children to look after and can't provide a one-child support service all the time. Would it be better for me to stay with him at kindy for as many sessions as it takes until he is playing happily with other children? Or should I be firm and drop him off as quickly as I can? I also question whether it is all a 'put on' to make Mum feel guilty, or a sign he is genuinely unhappy and perhaps has difficulties socialising?

A: I agree with you that too many changes and transitions can rattle a child's confidence. Let's assume his response to your leaving is not a 'put on to make Mum feel guilty' or a sign he has difficulty socialising, but rather is an indication he is struggling with being left at kindy. There are two possible explanations and you will need to ask the teachers what happens after you have left. One explanation is that if he is unhappy for a long time after you leave, or for the entire session, it is because he is struggling to manage without you. You might like to consider staying for a while for a few sessions. Take something to do, i.e. book, writing pad, laptop, knitting, whatever, and sit down at the side of the main playroom and get busy. Your son is welcome to bring toys to play next to you and it would be great if the teachers could invite him to join activities after he has settled and is convinced you are staying. You stay put. Let him have the experience of going off to play, running back to check you are there and then going off again secure in the knowledge he can return whenever he needs. Offer wordless cuddles. Be boring. Once he is spending the majority of time away from you, you can take the next step of leaving. The other explanation is if he is unhappy for a few minutes after you leave and then settles, then the cause is because he is anxious about the moment of separation. Therefore you need to make the separation fast (so you don't prolong the agony) and safe (so he has someone to comfort him). Don't try to settle him. Find his favourite teacher, if he has one. If you're not sure, ask him, 'Who would you like to cuddle you while Mum leaves?' Hand him over, kiss him goodbye and go. He may get very upset but he will be in the arms of someone who is going to be there for the duration of the session and who will be able to comfort him and engage him in play.

Diane Levy

mum and dad going away

Q: I would greatly appreciate some advice on how to handle an upcoming three-week absence from my toddler. My son is two and a half years old and is used to his parents being away for a night or two, having a babysitter stay at our house or staying with his grandmother at her house. But the next trip will be for three weeks and his maternal grandparents, whom he does not know well, are coming to stay in his house and look after him. I have no doubt he will adapt fine, especially as they are arriving four days before Mum and Dad leave but I am unsure whether I should tell him how long we will be away, allow him to cross days off a calendar, or just keep it all low-key and not mention it. Is it advisable to phone frequently whilst we are away to talk to him?

A: Three weeks is a long time for you to be away from your toddler and I am sure you are going to miss him a great deal. It is not predictable how he is going to react to your absence and you have made many excellent arrangements to make things as smooth as possible. Arrange it so that every day he can go down to the letterbox and find a 'letter' and a tiny treat (like a marshmallow or a packet of raisins or a small toy) waiting for him. I suggest that there is a picture and a brief message e.g. 'Here is a picture of a big lion, just for you. Love Mum and Dad.' His grandparents might like to set up a scrapbook that he can put the pictures in. Also, leave behind for him, a photo of the three of you. A calendar is a lovely idea but, at his age, it may be of no interest or relevance, so be prepared to drop it if it doesn't work. Similarly with phone calls. You will probably need to hear about him each day. He may have very little to say, so be prepared to sing him his favourite nursery rhyme even if or until he runs off bored. Anticipate that, when you return, he may be clingy for a while and not let you out of his sight.

Diane Levy

dawdling.

dawdling – hurry up please

We've all been there and it drives us crazy! For the past half an hour, as you race around the house getting everything ready to go out, you've asked your child over and over again to do one simple thing – to find her shoes and put them back on again . . . please . . . now! You are now late and the shoes are still nowhere to be seen!

The reassuring truth is that you are not alone in your frustration. Dawdling and being easily distracted is entirely normal in your child's early years.

There are a few reasons dawdling occurs. First, of course, she will take longer to get ready than you because she has far less experience and her motor skills are less developed. Second, due to her short attention span, what you say to your child often slips her mind seconds after you have said it. Your child lives in the moment, enjoying whatever may be of interest without much thought for what's to come.

Her young mind's view of the world is limited and often

based only on what concerns her. Even though she clearly heard you say, 'Hurry along, I have to leave soon,' she is easily distracted. The world is such an interesting place to her, it's easy for her to find something that takes her attention away from getting ready. The fact that you got frustrated minutes ago because she wasn't ready has slipped her mind once again.

Getting ready is meaningless and unimportant to her and she has little understanding of your need to rush and be on time. Consequently, she sees little reason to hurry up. 'What about just to help me?' I hear you ask your child. It's time for you to accept it – young children are egocentric! They view the world based on how it affects them, not on how it affects others. Having said all this, there are ways for you to ease the frustration.

get her attention

Get physically close to your child when talking to her. You may have to hold her hands and look into her face to make sure that she is focused on you and nothing else. Young children are often in their own world and don't pay attention to what's being said. Make eye contact with her, and speak to her in a firm and serious tone of voice in order to give her the message that what you're saying
is important.

speak calmly and respectfully

Your message will actually have more impact if you deliver it calmly and respectfully. It is also important that you speak to her with respect in order to teach her to respect you and to nurture your bond and her self-esteem.

Control your anger and communicate your feelings using an 'I' message, avoiding the temptation to use belittling phrases.
example: 'I get really frustrated when you ignore me.'

What parents may think of as dawdling and being easily distracted, may be seen as entirely normal to a young child. A young child can't tell the time so they have no sense of urgency.

instead of ...	try this ...
'It's time to get ready.'	'Please come here now and put your clothes on.'
'Put your pyjamas in the laundry basket and your slippers in your cupboard and then come and put your pants and shirt on.'	'Put your pyjamas in the laundry basket.' When she has done this say, 'Now put your slippers in your cupboard.' Once this is done, say, 'Come and put your pants and shirt on.'
'Would you just listen to me!'	'I don't think that you can put your top and pants on by the time the buzzer goes off!'

rather than: 'You're so silly.'
Avoid negative tactics such as being sarcastic, blameful, criticising, ridiculing, or putting her down. Rather than motivating her to do as you say, these are more likely to make her want to defy you.

tell her exactly what you want

Be specific. Your instructions need to be to the point, not complicated. Avoid vague directions such as, 'Get ready now.' Instead say, 'I need you to put your pants and socks on.'

limit instructions

Young minds cannot take in more than one or two instructions at a time. And with her limited memory, she is likely to forget if you ask for any more. Instead, go through each instruction progressively.

minimise distractions

The more there is around her to distract her, the slower she is likely to be. Find an area in your home for her to get ready where she will have few or no distractions.

incentivise

Use the 'when-then' rule ('When you are dressed, then you can play') or make an incentive-based rule ('If you are ready by 8:00 a.m. on the clock, you will have a few minutes to watch a video').

play games and reward

Make it fun for her to hurry up by getting her to race against you or the clock or buzzer. When you can, reward her with a privilege.

Praise her improvements, then she is more likely to hurry up for you next time.

think ahead, with a smile

- To ease your morning rush, prepare ahead as much as you can (i.e. the night before), have a consistent routine, guide your child through the routine and give yourself enough time.

- Shouting may work on the spur of the moment but fails to work if used repeatedly because your child is likely to feel angry and not want to please you.

- If you feel like shouting, wait a few seconds and/or take a few deep breaths before responding to your child.

- If your child refuses to comply with you, give her a consequence.

- Give her more attention when she is hurrying than when she is slowing down.

- You are better off allocating more time to her getting ready than repeatedly getting disappointed and frustrated.

Your young child does not dawdle on purpose. Rushing is simply the last thing on her mind. By planning ahead and guiding her with simple instructions and incentives – and doing it with a smile of gratitude because your child is just being a child – you do actually run the chance of reducing your frustration!

Chantal Gazal, Registered Psychologist

the wanderer

How can we wander-proof our children and stop them walking off? And going away on holiday can make it even harder to keep children in tow.

I can still clearly remember the day when my then 18 month old ran onto the road. I had picked her up from daycare and was busy carrying her still-dripping art masterpiece, her jacket, her bag, my bag, and my car keys – the normal things we parents carry out of daycare.

I had paused to open the car door, pop her things inside and turned to put my daughter into her car seat. In that time, she had dashed out behind me, around to the front of the car and was heading onto the middle of the road. A car swerved and missed her and thankfully everything else. I grabbed her, jammed her into her car seat, drove home alternating between yelling and shaking, gave her lunch, popped her into her cot for her afternoon sleep and burst into tears – then I sat down for a jolly good think about prevention.

'show me' instead of 'don't'

I had read quite recently that most children harmed in running-onto-the-road accidents had been growled at for the same offence within one week prior to the accident. So clearly I had to think of some other way to keep her safe. I embarked on

a programme of positive education using, 'Show me' instead of, 'Don't'. I would point to a line on our car and say, 'Show me how you can keep your hand on that line while I pack the car.' Wherever we went, I would be on the lookout for a positive anchor point. 'Show me how you can hang onto that little branch while I take your pushchair out of the car.'

It certainly didn't guarantee safety, but it did buy me a few spare seconds as long as I ladled in lots of recognition. 'Wow! You are hanging on so nicely. What a good girl.'

show boundary lines

Another lesson I found very useful was to teach her how far she was allowed to go. I showed her the line at the edge of the driveway – you can use chalk, or tape if there isn't a natural boundary line – and showed her that she could run up to that line and stop. Then she showed – many, many, many times! – that she knew how to run up and stop.

I ladled on the recognition and praise, and we showed aunty, grandma, and even the postman how marvellous she was. It didn't mean she could play near a road unsupervised, but it did mean she was much less likely to dash into danger.

don't say 'don't'

Try to put things into the affirmative rather than the negative. Get rid of the word 'Don't' from your vocabulary. For some unknown reason, children have a blocking system in their outer ear that prevents the word 'Don't' from being heard!

As parents we are always saying, 'Don't let go of my hand', 'Don't run across the road', and, 'Don't leave the playground area'. Apparently they hear, 'Let go of my hand', 'Run across the road', and, 'Leave the playground area'. Or at least that's the way they behave! You are better off saying, 'Show me how hard you can squeeze my hand', 'Show me how you stop at the kerb', and, 'Let's walk around the edge of the playground so you can see how far you are allowed to run. Now you show me.'

holidays make it harder

Start holiday-proofing your child several weeks ahead of travelling. Start treating run-away behaviour as a big 'no-no', right up there with hitting, biting and other unacceptable behaviours. Make a very clear distinction between a game of 'chase' and running off when you want to dress them, come to the dinner table, walk next to you, get in the car and so on. Start every game of 'chase' by announcing a

playful, 'I'm gonna get you', or whatever expression makes it clear that you have an agreement from both of you that you are playing a game.

If your child runs away from you at home when you make a specific request, don't chase him. Just get busy. Sooner or later he will show up next to you. Anchor him, scoop him up and put him in time out, saying very, very firmly, 'You know you are not allowed to run away from me.'

In the days leading up to your holiday, pay special attention to your child's behaviour. While you are still at home, insist on regular bedtimes, decent manners and a reasonable level of compliance.

When you get to your holiday destination, go for a walk around the site with your child, showing him where the boundaries are, where he may go, where he may only go supervised. Get him to show you and as many other adults as possible what he has learned, and be very impressed.

Think ahead as to what you will use as a time out spot if necessary. Remember a time out spot is anywhere you take your child, leave or hold him without further words or interaction, and allow him to leave when he is ready to behave in a civilised fashion.

If you expect good behaviour, demand good behaviour, and then be prepared to enjoy a wonderful fun time with a pleasant child who is a delight to be with.

Diane Levy, Family Therapist

worrying.

fears and scares

It's unlikely any of us will get through parenting our children without having to deal with them suddenly developing a catastrophic fear of something. Sometimes we may know how the fear started; other times it may pop up out of the blue.

There are many common childhood fears (our children may have none, some or all of them) – spiders, the dark, vacuum cleaners, night time monsters, thunder, the bath, going to the hairdresser or doctor, sudden loud noises. And then there are quirky ones, particular to our own child.

When our child is afraid, they may cry or get angry, become more dependent or start acting like a baby. However fears start and whatever they are, they create a situation that needs dealing with. It's important to take our child's fears seriously and to reassure them there is nothing to be frightened of, that we are there to keep them safe and to explain the situation to them. Most children will 'get it' if they are going to after the third or fourth explanation. So if being rational hasn't worked by then, it's not likely to. More than five repeats of the same explanation and you are nagging rather than helping.

distractions and bribes

Sometimes the offer of a distraction or bribe – a story, toy or game – is a quick and efficient way of getting our child through an awkward moment. If this works, great, but if it doesn't, a bigger or brighter one is unlikely to work any better, therefore, avoid making repeated and increasing offers. So, if the simple and obvious stuff hasn't worked, what next?

comfort and support

Just because the fear doesn't seem rational to you, it is very, very real to your child. Joking or teasing them out of it is not appropriate and rarely works. Belittling their fears is outright unkind. Instead, take them into your arms and say:

- You are really scared of that dog barking at the end of the street.
- You really don't like getting into your bath all of a sudden.
- After your injection, you are pretty scared of being in the doctor's waiting room.

Put your child's fears into words, whether or not they are verbal enough to do it for themselves. Then reassure, 'We are going to find a way of making it safe for you.'

safe times and places

If possible, go back to a position where your child felt safe and let them experience the fear this way several times before taking small steps towards the ordinary behaviour you are aiming for.

For instance, your child used to like dogs until an enthusiastic puppy bowled them over. Now when a dog barks, even though your child is safely inside the house, they panic shouting, 'No doggie. No doggie.' For the next several times this happens, pick your child up off the ground, cuddle, and support their feelings by saying, 'You don't like to hear that dog barking.' Hold them until they feel reassured and ready to get down. If you see a dog when you're out, prepare yourself for a long cuddle, give brief verbal support and keep cuddling. If you have access to a placid dog, let your child be in the same room at the other end. Go back for another visit and let them pat the dog's back.

It's important to take our child's fears seriously and to reassure them there is nothing to be frightened of, that we are there to keep them safe and to explain the situation to them.

The next time your child is fearful about something, remind them of a fear they have conquered, 'Remember when you were scared of the bath and you got brave and fixed that fear? Let's find a way of doing it with this one.'

For other fears, you may have to go back even further. Your child, having been happily bathed in an adult bath since they could sit, suddenly refuses to go near it. For a few days, you may need to revert to using a plastic wash-tub. When your child feels safe, move the tub to the bathroom, and then move the tub into the bath, and eventually put the plug in and have some water around the tub while your child sits in it.

If your child has a fear of going to the doctor, dentist or hairdresser, make an appointment for a social visit. Tell your child you are just going there to look and to say, 'Hello.' If possible, let them see some of the equipment and explain how it works. Be prepared for your child wanting to spend quite some time with their head buried in your shoulder before they are willing to trust people.

Role-play at home. This helps your child to know what to expect and introduces equipment that may be used – but don't pretend it won't hurt if it will as this will make your child more fearful next time. For haircutting fears, polystyrene cups with a painted face and cress seed growing on top are a great way for children to give something else haircuts.

small steps

Starting from where our child feels safe and letting them take small steps towards conquering their fears gives them valuable lessons for life. They experience parental support and kindness, learn to respect fears rather than dismiss them, and discover adults in their world can be trusted. Most importantly, children will experience the joy of mastering something they find difficult and can be justifiably proud of their efforts.

Almost all children experience fear at some stage and with your support and understanding, you can help them successfully overcome it.

Diane Levy, Family Therapist

pet fear

Q: Our four year old daughter is terrified of cats and dogs. While we can understand her fear of dogs, we are at a loss as to how to deal with her fear of cats. We have explained to her that cats won't hurt her and she has nothing to fear. We have encouraged her to be around cats so she can see how they act. But as soon as one comes near her, she screams and shakes and can't be calmed until the cat has gone. Her fear is so bad she always asks before we go out if a dog or cat will be there. It is also starting to affect how our younger child (aged two) acts around animals. We thought about getting a cat but one of us is allergic to cats. How can we help her overcome this fear?

A: You may have more success if you begin by expressing her feelings rather than trying to talk her out of them. For example you could say, 'You don't like being around cats just now, do you?' and, 'When we go somewhere, you worry there might be a cat there?' This way you are all on the same team and she can trust you to understand. The next step is to gradually get her to be familiar around cats so her fear doesn't get in the way of her going out. Get her some fluffy cat toys for cuddliness and familiarity – if you can find ones that 'meow' or 'purr', so much the better. Also check your library for books about cats. When you go to friends' houses, ring ahead and ask if they would mind their cat being outside while you are there. If you are extra lucky, you may get a lovely old cat asleep outside a window or ranch slider, far enough away from your daughter but close enough for her to clearly see it while being confident the cat can't get to her. Cats that run away as soon as visitors arrive can also be a wonderful way for your daughter to learn to feel powerful around cats. If you can, go back to visit and I would guess by the third time, she might even like to try stroking the cat. The important part of the process is for you to acknowledge and support her fears and step-by-step help her go from looking at pictures and playing with soft toys to being around cats to actually touching them. While she may never be crazy about cats or dogs, all you need is for her to tolerate them socially.

Diane Levy

fear of monsters

Q: I have two boys nearly three and four years old. I have been doing the 'pop-in' method to try and get them to sleep at night without me being right there with them. My youngest boy is fine with me not being in the room, but my eldest is far more sensitive and says he has a fear of monsters and that he needs me. I think because I had a bad fear of the dark and other spooky things in my childhood, I give in and feel for him. What can I say and do to make it ok?

A: I would warmly recommend making him a 'Bravery Kit' to help him deal with the fear that there may be monsters. Get a shoe box and place in it a soft toy, a torch and a 'weapon'. The soft toy is for comfort. The torch is to light up any dark corners and to check that there are no monsters in the room. (Stock up on lots of batteries or get rechargeable ones.) Which 'weapon' to choose is a matter of what you think your son would find most effective. Some children like to have a gun or a sword. Others prefer wands that glow in the dark, straws to blow them away or even a small, hand-held fan. I favour quiet weapons! Every bedtime, give him his bravery kit and run through the items. 'Here is your cuddly toy to keep you company, here is your torch to shine in the corners and frighten away the monsters (they're scared of light) and here is your weapon to scare the monsters off.' If some time later, he calls out that he is scared, just go in and tell him, here is your bravery kit. Let's check you've still got everything you need to take care of monsters.

Diane Levy

haircut fear

Q: When my nearly four year old son has a haircut, you would think that we were the cruellest parents around. He finds it absolutely intolerable and gets extremely hysterical. I am not sure if it is the scissors, being draped in black capes, or the entire thought of getting his haircut! How can I make it more pleasant for all of us! I feel I have tried everything.

A: The odds are you have tried offering every form of reward and have also spent a lot of time explaining to him how it is not going to hurt and it will be over soon. It would be worth tackling it from another angle by first giving him empathy and then turning the problem over to him and offering him support for his solutions. Try starting with, 'I know you really, really scared of having your hair cut but it is all different lengths and we need to get them evened out.' Next ask him what he needs to be able to handle it. 'What can I do to help you while you are having your hair cut?' I find that this way of tackling things is very respectful of our children and I never cease to be amazed how often our children come up with some simple support that will help them through a difficult time.

Diane Levy

tantrums.

I wa-a-ant it!

How many of us begin our supermarket shopping with, 'If you're really good you'll get a treat afterwards,' only to have the entire expedition accompanied by a stream of questions – What sort of treat? When can I have it? Can I have it now? – and on and on!

After giving our children a perfectly nutritious breakfast, how many of us find them trailing along behind us shortly afterwards whining, 'I want a biscuit?' 'I want a banana!' How often do we try to get tasks done to the sounds of, 'I want you to play with me!'

under the radar

Continuous demanding is one of those behaviours that is insidious and tends to stay under the radar until we eventually realise it has been going on and on and on and we suddenly find ourselves shouting. When we pause and reflect, we may feel we have set up an expectation, or rule, by giving our children treats at the supermarket, by giving them chips or biscuits on a whim, by stopping what we are doing to play with them.

All these activities are perfectly reasonable and often delightful parental behaviour – we should feel free to give our children treats when we like, to give them the odd snack, or to play with them just because it's fun.

But what can we do when delight turns into demand, and 'occasional' turns into a tyrannical rule?

The first thing that may help us deal with a demanding child is to distinguish the difference between need and want. 'I need a treat. I need a drink. I ne-e–e-d someone to play with,' is a want in disguise. It is unlikely health or quality of life will suffer if you don't give into these particular types of needs.

it's okay to change the rules

Often, when we are giving in to yet another demand, we are aware that we set ourselves up. But we make excuses for ourselves by saying we started it, so it doesn't feel fair to stop it. It all began innocently enough, or, just one more won't hurt. We gave our child a packet of chippies. We stopped what we were doing and played with our child. We gave our child a treat to keep him busy while we were shopping. Now suddenly it seems to be a rule (to our children that is) that we have to obey every time or we can expect trouble.

This is no time to succumb to helpless guilt – of course we can offer nice things to our children but just because we do it once, twice, or even a few times, doesn't make it a rule or that it will happen every time. Even though we set the rules up, when we do change one of them, you can expect there will be some fuss.

broken record

Decide very clearly in your own head what the old rule has been, and what the new rule will be. Be prepared to employ the 'broken record' technique.

A long time ago, before CDs and MP3s, the only way of listening to recorded music was with records. If the record was scratched in any way, the record needle

How many of us feel like, 'If I get one more "I want it", I'm going to scream?'

105

Holiday times are a great time to bite the bullet and change the custom. Hopefully, we are under a little less time pressure and have the space to clearly see there might be a problem, the energy to think up a strategy and the time and strength to let the inevitable wobblies play themselves out.

got stuck and it would go round and round in the same spot, and you listened to the same phrase over and over. And so the 'broken record' technique was born. Pick one phrase and be prepared to repeat it over and over again, politely and kindly, until your child gets the message.

You are about to go to the supermarket. Announce, 'Let's have morning tea before we go because there are not going to be any treats while we are there.' While you are shopping, with every demand, just say, 'No treats. We are here only to shop.'

Your child comes to you two seconds after breakfast and demands a biscuit. Get out your broken record, 'Biscuits are for morning and afternoon tea only.' Repeat as necessary. At morning tea, produce the biscuit.

You begin the morning tidy-up. Two little figures appear next to you and demand you play with them. Be prepared to repeat, 'First I am going to do the dishes and make the beds. Then I am going to play with you,' as many times as necessary.

story from home

When my children were little, as a matter of survival, I made it a rule that after supermarket shopping, they were welcome to sit and bounce on any 'novelty ride' conveniently located just outside the supermarket, but I was never going to put a coin in.

My daughter-in-law recently asked her son (age two and a half) to tell Grandma what he did at the supermarket that day. He enthused, 'Ride on Bert and Big Bird.' My two children (now both adults), turned to me and accused in unison, 'We were never allowed a ride at the supermarket!'

Diane Levy, Family Therapist

temper tantrums

Whenever I am in a supermarket and see an angry or despairing child plaster themselves onto the floor and begin wailing and screaming, I immediately think, 'Oh your poor thing! Who on earth is ever going to come to your rescue?'

By the way, the 'poor thing' I am fretting about is you, the parent! We've all had that awful moment when our child goes ballistic and out of control and we have that nagging feeling that a 'good' parent would be able to prevent the tantrum in the first place.

The reality is that no one can continuously prevent a child from getting terribly upset or angry. However, sometimes when we sense that our child is winding up, we can do things that will head off the major wobbly. Other times, there is nothing that we can do but weather it.

Tantrums are not created equal. There are two sorts of tantrums - tantrums of despair and tantrums of control. If we can recognise what sort of tantrum it is that we are dealing with, we can be more effective in helping our children deal with the feelings that overwhelm them – and which also threaten to overwhelm us.

tantrums of despair

Sometimes our children are dreadfully upset. The square peg

won't go into the round hole; they expected to go play in the park and now it is raining; Mum said, 'No' to a third chocolate biscuit; their friend just doesn't want to play with them; they just knocked their shin on the corner of the chair. Our child may be tearful, angry or both.

First, let's talk about the things that don't work well. Logical and reasoned explanations are of little help when our child is overwhelmed by feelings and unable to think. Trying to calm her down and suggesting it is not worth so much fuss is not helpful when our child is revving up to full volume. Distraction may sometimes work but is usually very hard work for the parent.

What our children need is for us to say something that shows them we understand how upset they are. It is comforting to our children to have us put into words what they are feeling. If we are to be really convincing we need to use our tone of voice to match the intensity of their feelings.

'That puzzle just won't go right for you, will it!'

'You are so disappointed that it is raining and we can't go to the park.'

'You really, really wanted another biscuit but it is too close to dinner.'

'You are so upset that your friend doesn't want to play right now.'

'Ouch! Your shin must really, really hurt.'

Having said this, there is little else to add to the subject. Now is the time to offer, 'Do you need a cuddle?' or the time-honoured magic approach of, 'Can Mummy kiss it better?' Just keep your arms around your child, don't say anything other than a few soothing sounds and wait. Pretty soon your child will have got over it and be ready for the next adventure.

tantrums of control

Sometimes our strong willed children will use a tantrum of anger to try to force us to change our mind. They are more likely to scream rather than cry. They may squirm and wriggle to get away while being changed. If they cannot get their own way through shouting or running, they may resort to hitting, shoving, spitting, or yelling unkind or unacceptable words.

At this point, we often resort to threats of punishment if the behaviour continues. The problem with this approach is that it would need our child to be in a calm, thinking state to be able to understand the consequences of where his behaviour might be leading him. But, a yelling child is rarely able to hear us above his own noise. A thinking child we need to respond to a tantrum of control with distance rather than empathy. It may be easiest to walk away or it may be necessary to pop him in a separate room.

Either way, there is little point in arguing or reasoning. Our children are too enraged to listen to what we have to say. It is much more effective to forget about negotiating and to pop our child in a quiet space to calm down. If our child is too

despair or control?

How can we tell if we are dealing with a tantrum of despair or a tantrum of control? The simplest way is to check our own feelings. If our first thought is, 'You poor little thing,' then the odds are that it is a tantrum of despair and our child needs our support.

If our initial feeling is one of anger, or if we feel pushed around by our small 'monster', then the odds are high that it is a tantrum of control. We are better off distancing ourselves from our child until he is ready to concede control and see it our way.

still not sure?

If you are still not sure, try empathy first. 'Do you need a

It took me a long time to understand that having a lovely time can also be very exhausting for our children and when their tiredness catches up, they simply 'lose the plot'.

cuddle?' If it is a tantrum of despair, your child will come into your arms for some comfort.

If it is a tantrum of control, he is more likely to yell, 'Go away! I don't like you!' This is the signal to create some distance between you – either by your going way or by placing him into a Time Out space.

Many children, after a few minutes on their own, will switch from anger to upset and it is appropriate for us to match their feelings by offering them a cuddle if they are now ready for one.

too much in one day

The third type of tantrum often occurs when our child is overtired, overstimulated or both. This often comes after a perfectly lovely outing or party when our child has had an excellent time. They have been charming and delightful and everyone has told us how gorgeous they are.

At the moment of departure, suddenly they turn into a hideous, whirling dervish of flailing arms and legs and temper. What went wrong? How could they behave so badly when we have spent considerable effort to give them such a good time.

In these situations there is no magic answer. Often we just have to get through the situation as best we can. A nice calming bath, a quiet story time, a good night's sleep and our child will wake up ready to be their usual charming selves. They are likely to behave as if nothing happened. We, however, may still be shattered!

Diane Levy, Family Therapist

out & about

You're on your way to the pharmacy when your child spots a toy in a shop window and stubbornly refuses to go any further; you're at the supermarket with one child trying to climb out of the trolley while the other is racing; there's a queue a mile long at the Post Office and you must get a parcel posted today, but your child is showing signs of a massive tantrum.

Going out will never be the same again once you have a toddler. He is likely to touch things he shouldn't, move around when he's supposed to sit still, or get restless because he is not busy enough.

Nevertheless, there are ways to make outings with him easier and more enjoyable for everyone.

have realistic expectations

Your child is not a miniature adult. You cannot expect him to be quiet and co-operative while you shop for hours. He needs to be kept stimulated, interested and busy a great deal of the time; otherwise problems will inevitably occur.

Consider your child's needs before planning your outing. If you need to go shopping for a long time, consider hiring a babysitter, dropping your child at a relative's for a few hours or even shopping online or by catalogue.

plan ahead

Think about how you will keep him busy when you are away from home. Plan on how you will handle his difficult behaviour if it occurs.

Explain to him exactly what's to come: 'We are going to the cafe, then to the toy shop. Later we will stop at the park for a play.'

Clarify exactly what is expected of him. 'In the café, you must use your quiet voice only. Your bottom must be on the chair when you're eating.' 'At the toy shop, I am only buying a present for your cousin Jack's birthday. We are not buying one for you today.' You may also ask for his input, 'What is not allowed at the cafe?' 'What happens if you ask me for a treat?' Then clarify any wrong answers.

shorter is better

Shorter trips may seem like a hassle, but breaking outings into shorter segments means your children are more likely to be better behaved. Limit shopping time to one or two hours at a time. Break it up with a fun activity such as stopping at the pet shop, going to the park, or having a special lunch.

keep him busy

Do something together or keep his mind occupied with something he enjoys whenever you can.

choose your timing

Avoid going shopping when your child may be tired or hungry, or going to a café or restaurant when it is extremely busy and you have to wait a long time to be served.

notice positive behaviour

Whenever his behaviour is good, thank or praise him. Be specific, 'Thank you for keeping busy with your cards and letting me talk to the salesperson,' so he knows exactly what he did right.

Don't make the mistake of ignoring your child if he is quiet and well behaved, and only paying attention to him when he misbehaves. This signals to him that he is more likely to get you to notice him if he misbehaves, thus opening the door for troublesome behaviour.

be prepared to discipline

Be prepared to discipline him as you do at home. If you discipline your child less, or not at all, when you are out in order to keep the peace, this teaches him that he can get away with certain behaviours when he is not at home. Although this strategy may seem like the most effective and easiest one at the time, it is more likely to lead to problem behaviours. Enforce limits as you would at home. Go outside to follow through on a consequence (time out in the car) or go home if your child gets unruly. Even though it may be a hassle the few times it occurs, he won't like it and it won't take long before his behaviour improves generally.

If necessary, set up a reinforcement programme. If you have tried the above strategies and you are still struggling to keep your child well behaved, set up a reward programme for the particular problem behaviour. For example, if he keeps running away from you when you're out, offer him a small treat or toy at the end of a shopping trip if he stays near you the whole time.

when you're out

An essential skill for any family outing is finding a way to keep your little one busy and happy. Before you leave, pack a bag with a snack, small treasured toy, books, pack of crayons or coloured pencils, notepad, pack of cards, and/or electronic toy like a calculator (to keep little fingers busy).

waiting at the doctor's office

- Play I-Spy for an object of a certain colour.
- Draw an item on paper and let him guess what it is.
- Teach him about different coins. Have him close his eyes and guess the coin you put in his hand.
- Play 'Guess who I am' and give him hints.
- Practise numbers on a calculator or just let him have fun pushing the buttons.
- If space prevails, lay out a pack of cards and let him sort them into colours or by numbers.

shopping trips

- Have a list of errands to run and items to buy to make your trip short and efficient.
- Have him find items (bananas, a certain cereal) for you. Let him give money to the teller.
- When waiting at the cash register, ask him which items are edible and which are not.
- If your child is interested in a toy, ask him to put it on his birthday or Christmas wish list.
- Look for signs of an impending meltdown and make sure to leave before.

Chantal Gazal, Registered Psychologist

at a café or restaurant

- Choose a venue that is child-friendly and where making a mess and noise won't upset others.
- Ensure your child's food is brought out before or at the same time as yours.
- Ask for some bread straightaway to ease his hunger.
- Make rubbings of items (coins, credit cards etc.) by putting the object under a piece of paper and running a crayon over it.
- Make objects using twist ties.

waiting in a queue

- Give him a book or magazine to read.
- Bring out the snack (small packets of food are far more interesting!).
- Crouch down to his level and tell him a funny story – keep asking him to guess what comes next to keep up curiosity.

whining & grizzling

There are days when our littlies seem to be able to take everything in their stride, and others when they seem to do nothing but whine and grizzle. Perhaps the most difficult of all is the child who seems to whine all day and nothing seems to make them happy.

When a usually cheerful or generally placid child is whiney, there is something bothering them and often with some cuddling and comforting, they will tell you or show you what the problem is. Usually you're able to fix it or at least offer an alternative that will satisfy them.

With children who are sensitive and easily upset, they will often settle with a cuddle and some low-key time engaged in a pleasant activity. But with strong willed children, who seem determined to remain miserable and make everyone around them suffer, we need to make it clear that we will not be part of their resolve to have a bad day.

We don't need to tolerate the whining of a child who can communicate most needs (whether verbally or non-verbally) but resists all our attempts to find out what the problem is or to support them while they are feeling miserable. You will notice that I haven't said, 'Our attempts to cheer them up.' We place too great an expectation upon ourselves when we wish to 'make

them happy'. This lays us wide open to taking responsibility for the feelings of a child who is not cheerful by nature, and to engage in the near impossible just to get a smile or a laugh out of a child who doesn't feel that way inclined.

So if you cannot – or should not – jolly him out of his whining and it is driving you crazy, what are your options? Don't wait until it is driving you crazy. Start early and intervene in the whining behaviour before you get too angry to handle it calmly.

First, check your own feelings. Do you feel sorry for him? Or are you already at the, 'Oh for heaven's sake', stage? If you feel sorry for him, the odds are that some emotional support, such as a cuddle, is called for. If you feel frustrated or angry, then a bit of emotional distance, such as time out, is the best way to go.

distracting is hard – try once

Our children often whine when we have to say 'No' to them. It's ten minutes before dinner and they want a biscuit. Even though we've explained they can't have one, they still whine, 'I want a biscuit!'

Often we try to diffuse this by offering a consolation, 'There'll be a chance of some more tomorrow.' We may try offering an alternative, 'Would a crunchy stick of celery help?', or we may begin growling, 'Oh for heaven's sake, will you stop that whining!' Or our child might just be trailing us around whining and clinging.

We try hard to suggest other activities in the hope they will get involved and distracted, but they seem grimly determined to keep on whining. Feel free to give up on reasoning and distracting after the first attempt. If the strategy is not going to work on the first attempt, it is unlikely to work on the fifth. Also, reasoning and distracting are much too much like hard work.

Children whine and grizzle for a variety of reasons - often when they are feeling tired, hungry or even overwhelmed. Sensitive and easily upset children will often settle with a cuddle but strong willed children can make everyone around them miserable.

parents need space too!

It is perfectly reasonable to decide that whining for whining's sake is unacceptable behaviour and you won't tolerate it. If you have offered distractions, support and space and your child is still trailing you around whining, it's more than likely (and perfectly natural) that you'll be getting angry.

give emotional support

Turn to your little whiner, put your arms out and say, 'Are you a big boy who needs a cuddle?' If your child accepts a cuddle, stand still or even better, sit down and say very sympathetically, 'You are really feeling very miserable.'

After that, there is not much left to say. Hold still. Be soothing and extremely boring, and stay there until your child has finished feeling miserable and goes to find something more interesting to do. You may need to do this several times. Although these might be frustrating interruptions to what you are doing, you are giving your child an opportunity to sort it out for himself in a safe pair of arms as well as your not trying to do the impossible – trying to make him happy.

If your offer of a cuddle is met with an angry response, 'No, go away! I don't like you!,' or any other response that indicates your offer of a cuddle is not appreciated, it may be that your child needs some space to sort himself out. Either move off and get busy in another part of the room or house, or scoop him up and take him to his room. As you put him into his room, say, 'You need a bit of time on your own. If you want a cuddle later, come and get it. I'll have saved one just for you.' Sit down for a 'cuppa' and a breather. Go back and check whether he has finished whining or decided to keep on going.

If he has finished whining, he is welcome to join the family. Remember, it is his decision to keep on whining and if he wishes to continue it, then he is better off whining in the privacy of his own room.

Diane Levy, Family Therapist

playing up when feeding the baby

Q: I have a two and a half year old girl and a six week old boy. My very clever two plus has figured out that I can't leap up when breastfeeding and so she sometimes behaves very badly. I don't want to make feeding time an unpleasant experience by shouting or creating tension, as I don't want my breastfeeding boy to 'go on strike'. Do I ignore the bad, presumably attention-seeking, behaviour? I don't want to exclude my little girl from feed times and I'm reluctant to put my little boy on and off the breast while I action time out, particularly since she has only recently toilet trained and on a couple of occasions has soiled or wet while she's in time out.

A: I sympathise with your dilemma about which need of which child to put first. It is not an easy one. Now that your baby is six weeks old, I would recommend risking interrupting a few of his feeds so that you can show your two and a half year old that you are not going to be held hostage to bad behaviour just because you are apparently 'trapped' feeding the baby. Before feeding the baby, take your daughter to the toilet (an empty bladder makes it slightly harder to wet in time out) and then help her pick a few toys that she would like to play with next to you while you feed the baby. As soon as she begins to behave badly, pop your baby down in a safe place and put your girl in time out and then finish the first half (or side) of the feed. Go back and offer her the opportunity to come out and play nicely for the second half of the feed. If she misbehaves again, pop her back in time out, finish the feed and then open her door and simply say, 'You are welcome out.' For children who repeatedly (and probably deliberately) wet or soil in time out, I recommend you use a time out spot in an area that is not carpeted.

Diane Levy

breaks and throws things

Q: My three and a half year old son has an aggressive side. He has broken most of his toys and a number of household items. When he doesn't get his way, he throws things around the house. I just don't know how to stop this behaviour. He seems to throw something on a daily basis and I am finding it very frustrating and don't know what I am doing wrong.

A: Strong willed children often get angry when Mum or Dad has to say 'No'. One of the things that our children have to learn is that parents need to say 'No' to inappropriate requests and that the child needs to be able to cope with the frustration of taking 'No' for an answer. When you have to say 'No' or insist on something being done, go right over to him and give him a combination of empathy and a clear instruction, 'I know you would like to have a biscuit now, but you need to wait until afternoon tea time.' If he accepts what you say, put an arm around him and say, 'That's a good boy.' If he refuses to accept what you have said – and you will know by his manner in seconds – and looks like he is about to create mayhem, scoop him up and pop him in his room. Tell him you will be back to see him when he is ready. Then you go back and ask, 'Are you ready to come out?' Either he is ready to come out and to behave, ready for a cuddle to settle his feelings (give him a cuddle), or not ready to behave in a civilized fashion. If the latter is the case, say to him, 'You are not quite ready. I'll pop back soon.'

Diane Levy

aggressive towards me

Q: My eldest son is very aggressive towards me and tells me he doesn't love me, sometimes even throwing his toys at me. He is only three years old, yet I don't know how to react when he says or does these things. Usually I just respond with, 'I love you, though', but he still persists. It mostly happens when he asks me to play with him but I can't because I'm busy and tell him that. For example, if I'm on the phone and he's standing next to me saying, 'I want to talk to the person on the phone,' I respond with, 'No! Please go and play with your cars, this is an important phone call.' He will insist on talking, I say, 'No', and then he says he doesn't love me. It really hurts. I know I'm doing something wrong and I don't want to ruin my son's beautiful personality.

A: Your letter says that your three year old responds to not getting his own way by being aggressive, by saying, 'I don't love you,' and by throwing toys at you. When you try to explain, he's not convinced by your explanation. I suggest you set aside times of the day (for quarter of an hour two or three times each day) that you do play with him and, if at all possible, don't answer the phone during that time. At other times, it is reasonable for you to expect him to occupy himself by working or playing alongside you, or going off and playing on his own. Teach him phone manners and when it is appropriate, let him say, 'Hello (Name) here. Here's my Mum,' and hand the phone back to you. Try a special 'playing quietly toy' that is only available to him when you are on the phone and you can keep within arm's reach of the phone. When the phone rings, hand it to him so he can play alongside you while you are talking. If none of these are powerful enough – and there will be times when it isn't appropriate for him to say hello – and he misbehaves while you are on the phone, you will need to take immediate action. Excuse yourself to the person on the phone, pick him up and put him in his room, or any other convenient spot. At the door, say, 'I can't hear with all that noise going on. I'll be back when I've finished on the phone.' Go back and complete the call. Open the door and say, 'I've finished. You're welcome to join me now.' No other comment is necessary.

Diane Levy

can't control his anger

Q: I'm a mother of two. I think my son is having a problem in controlling his anger. When he is angry he hits and pushes his sister, and even me. No matter how much I talk to him and advise him about this, the situation doesn't seem to be getting any better. What should I do to turn these angry situations into happy situations? It's very stressful. According to his kindy teachers, he is perfectly all right at kindy. I wonder why he only acts like this at home. Is he taking advantage of us, or is it something else? I'm worried that he might turn out to be violent.

A: Your son is perfectly all right at kindy and can control his anger there. Congratulations. You have done a good mothering job and have raised a son who is perfectly capable of not hitting. Now all you have to do is believe that if he is capable of stopping himself from hitting at kindy, he is perfectly capable of stopping himself at home. You have to show him that he is never allowed to hit or push at home. Give up on talking to him and advising him about it. I assume that he is normally bright and gets most things on the first, second or third explanation. We can assume that no amount of advising or explaining is going to get him to change his mind. Every time he hits or pushes, take him to his room. At the door, say very sternly, 'You know you are not allowed to hit! You can call me when you are ready to behave properly!' Do this every time he lashes out (whether it connects or not!) and pretty soon you are likely to have a child who can control his irritations at home as well as at kindy.

Diane Levy

won't leave willingly

Q: I have three boys aged five, three and 19 months and it seems every time we go to leave kindy, school, the park or shops they will not willingly leave with me. My youngest hates being held or strapped in and can get out of the pushchair but will hold hands if he wants to go with me. Neither is he the least bit worried if I go to leave or I'm out of his sight. I also don't have any hands free with the pushchair to control the other two. I will persuade two of them to come with me but while I am extracting the third the other two use that as a reason to dart off and go and play again or one will decide he urgently needs to go to the toilet at the exact point I am about to go out the gate.

A: I wish that I could tell you a magic trick that would work, or some amazing reward or punishment that would turn your children's behaviour around in an instant but I don't know of a 'quick fix'. You may find it useful to think of your children's behaviour as disobedient and disrespectful. I am sure they know that you expect them to come with you when you say so but they are not taking a bit of notice. I would start to pay attention to their level of compliance at home when you ask them to do something or to stop doing something. The reason for this is because at home you have much greater control and can teach them that you expect compliance to simple requests. If you have another of these ghastly departure scenes, get them home as best you can, tell them very clearly (with measured anger) that their behaviour was appalling. Pop them in their rooms and tell them you will come and find them when you are ready to see them. After a few experiences like that, they should be getting the message.

Diane Levy

toileting.

toilet training

Toilet training doesn't have to be a tug of war between you and your child. Rather than forcing your child to toilet train, it's far less stressful for everyone if you take a relaxed attitude and simply wait until they start to show signs of readiness.

Generally a child will show signs of toilet training readiness between 18 months and three years, but don't be concerned if your child is earlier or later than this – every child is different and will start when developmentally ready.

Check for one or all of the following signs of readiness:

Is your child able to stay dry for one or two hours at a time?

Is he showing signs that he is aware of the way his body works? That is, does he recognise when he has done wees or poos?

Does he have bowel movements around the same time every day?

Does he understand why others go to the toilet?

Does he have the co-ordination to dress and undress?

Does he like to imitate older children or adults?

Does he want to get rid of his nappy and to wear underpants?

Only when your child is showing signs of toilet training readiness should you start the toilet training process itself. You can start preparing him with some toilet training basics:

- Teach him toilet training words such as 'poo', 'wee', 'potty', 'dry', 'wet' and 'dirty'.

- Talk about how his body works and when he is doing poos, say, 'Sam is doing poos.'

- Explain using a doll or if you're comfortable, leave the door open so your child sees you going to the toilet.

- Encourage him to dress and undress himself as he will need to be able to do this with ease before you begin training.

- Get him used to following simple instructions such as, 'Give Mummy the book,' 'Come here,' and, 'Sit down.'

the process

- **get him into appropriate clothes and out of nappies**
  Choose clothing that is easy to put on and take off. He can wear a pull-up, training pants

Generally a child will show signs of toilet training readiness between 18 months and three years.

or underpants. The more he feels it when he goes, the quicker he will learn. In a pull-up nappy he will feel dry so that he will take longer to realise when he has a wee. In underpants, he will feel it right away but it will create a mess for you to clean up. With training pants, your child will feel it when he wees, but the mess won't be as much. It comes down to personal choice as to which method you use.

- **sit him on the potty**
  To start, get him used to sitting on the potty with clothing and then with his bare bottom. Do this slowly and gradually if he is reluctant at first. Once he is used to sitting on the potty, take him to it if he hasn't had a wee for a while, when you know that it's around his time to have a bowel movement or when you notice a familiar sign (e.g. jumping up and down, hiding in a corner).

- **keep him busy**
  He is less likely to get bored and restless if you read a book, tell him a story, sing songs or just talk to him.

- **don't force him**
  If he refuses to go, don't hurry him and don't insist. Rather, try again later. If he could go, he would. Learning to go when you ask akes time. Moreover, if you begin to make this a

power struggle he will be less likely to want to learn.

- **wait a few minutes or try again later**
  If he's not able to go after a few minutes, praise his attempt and train in half an hour's time.

Keep repeating the process, but relax and be patient, it will all happen in time. Trying to rush through the toilet training process will only create stress on you and your child. Like any acquired skill, toilet training takes time, practice and patience.

Every child is different so let your child guide you through the process. How long it will take depends on him. Your job as a parent or caregiver is to teach him the toilet training process, to provide the structure and routine he needs, and to let him lead while you guide and encourage. Punishing, lecturing or making your child feel ashamed of his accidents won't help. In fact, doing so is likely to work against you. Remember, your child is not 'naughty' when he has an accident; he just hasn't developed the control.

Calmly clean up the mess and focus on using positive strategies when he does succeed, and encourage him to try again next time when he doesn't.

Toilet training does not need to be a stressful or difficult experience and remind yourself not to worry because no-one goes to school in nappies!

Chantal Gazal, Registered Psychologist

Toilet training doesn't need to be a stressful or difficult experience and remind yourself not to worry because no-one goes to school in nappies!

weeing all over the house

Q: For the last couple of weeks my son aged three years, eight months has been urinating in the house – on the sofa, our bed (once) and mostly on the carpet in his room. This is done in a sneaky but purposeful way. At first I dealt with it calmly, he was given a cloth to clean up and told he would miss out on dessert and a story at bedtime. This happened three times. Then he missed out on swimming which really upset him. It still went on so we took a harder approach, a stern telling off and time out. Nothing is working and we are at our wits' end.

A: As parents we are often given advice to respond calmly, explain the problem and give the child a chance to participate in remedying the situation. This is entirely appropriate for childish accidents. It is completely inappropriate for deliberate and outrageous behaviour – and wee-ing deliberately (except in the toilet!) is one of those. We are also advised to growl at and punish inappropriate behaviour. Where this isn't working, it is because our child has decided that punishment gives him a choice. 'If I can withstand the growling and the punishment, then I am free to do that behaviour again.' I suggest that you decide, in your own mind, that this behaviour is unacceptable and won't happen in your household. Whenever he wees in the wrong spot, take him instantly to time out without a word until you get there. At the door say, 'You know that is unacceptable behaviour and we don't do that in this home. I've got a lot of cleaning up to do. You stay here.' Clean up and go back only when you are ready to see him again. Open the door and say, 'You can come out now,' and make no further comment. You know why he was there; he knows why he was there. There is nothing else left to say.

Diane Levy

his wee privates seem non-existent

Q: I am not sure if this is a common question – or whether I am just a nutty mum. My little man is two. Although he is full of beans and larger than most little children his age, I am worried about his 'wee privates'. They have never seemed to get any bigger – and in fact seem non-existent.

A: Usually an abnormally small penis is noticed at birth by your doctor or midwife, and if there is concern a referral is made then. Very rarely it indicates an endocrine (or glandular) problem. Subsequently, when the penis is noticed to be small, the commonest cause is that it is 'buried' in the fat above and around the penis. The experts measure the stretched penile length which should be above 2.5 cm at birth and 3.5 cm at two years of age. From six years of age, until the pubertal growth occurs, it remains at about 6 cm. It is likely that if your son is a big boy that his penis is 'buried' and will emerge normally as he grows up. It would be sensible to ask your doctor to have a look at him for reassurance.

Dr Simon Rowley

penis query

Q: This might be a strange query, but my nine month old son's penis never apparently moves or differs in appearance at all. With his nappy off, he has never done one of those wees which can go anywhere (which we are told to watch out for with boys). It just goes straight down. I also don't have to check that it is pointing down when putting nappies on because it is always in exactly the same place. I only notice this because it is so different from my first son's and other baby boys' I have seen. Is this anything to be concerned about?

A: What you describe is not uncommon. There is a large variation in the position and appearance of a baby boy's penis. Sometimes it can appear to be buried in the fat pad around the area but it will eventually emerge as it should. Some babies have erections just before passing urine and others don't. It would be sensible to have your doctor check your son to rule out any of the rare but minor malformations where there is tethering of the skin on the under-surface of the penis causing it to stay down (chordae). In these situations a small operation to release the tethering is all that is commonly necessary.

Dr Simon Rowley

refuses to do poos on the toilet

Q: I have a four year old boy who refuses to do poos on the toilet. He was easily toilet trained from around the age of two and has been fine doing wees. He knows when he needs to go poos and will complain of a sore tummy and then ask to have his nappy put on. I've refused to put the nappy on and I explained to him that he's a big boy and capable of doing poos on the toilet. The longest this battle went on was for a week, at which point I started to feel uncomfortable and eventually gave in and put the nappy on. Since then, I have stopped putting too much pressure on him but I'm not happy because I feel he's getting the message that refusal means having your nappy put on. He has a good diet, eats plenty of fruit. Please help.

A: As parents, we often assume that because our child can hold onto his wees and wait until he gets to the toilet or potty and let go in the right place, he will be able to do the same with his poos. Not always so! You were quite right to give up on refusing letting him have a nappy on. While it can work for some children, for others it can lead to a child hanging on for as long as it takes to get a private moment. I have known children to become very constipated or ill when parents have insisted they cannot have a nappy on. Your son knows when his body needs to go poos, can hang on until he gets to the right spot (in his mind, the right spot is his nappy!), and then let it go into his nappy. So in other words, he is toilet trained and the only argument is about the location. Here is how to get him to use a different location, i.e. the toilet. Week one – Get him back to the point when he can ask you for a nappy when he feels like doing poos. Help him put one on and after he has done it and asks to be changed, do so as pleasantly as you can manage. (A week is a rough guide. He needs several experiences of success at each stage before moving on to the next.) Week two – You put on his nappy when he asks for it but now he must go into the room where everybody poos (the toilet) and do his poos there. Week three – You still put his nappy on although now he teaches his body to sit on the toilet before pooing in his nappy. When he is finished, tell him he has done well and change him. Pretty soon after the third week, he will come out one day and announce that he has done poos in the toilet. Go celebrate.

Diane Levy

my baby screams when doing poos

Q: I'm a mother of two and it feels like my 11 month old son screams every day when he feels the need to do poos. He stiffens his whole body and then goes bright red as if he is trying to hold it in. Then the feeling passes and he returns to his usual happy self. He's been doing this since he was three months old. I always thought babies had no control of this – is it possible a three month old can have a fear of bowel movements? My paediatrician said it was normal and put him on laxatives, but he still screams whether or not we give him laxatives. My Plunket nurse, who witnessed one of his screaming fits, said she had never seen this before. I can't imagine the stress of this is very good for my son. I have tried everything from fruit to juices. Is this common in young children and how can I overcome the problem?

A: Your child has almost certainly had constipated stools at some stage (remember, constipation means very hard stools that are difficult and often painful to pass). As a result, he still remembers the uncomfortable sensation of passing a stool so that when his rectum is full, he strains to keep it in while at the same time having the need to push it out. This is very confusing for him and over time he associates the need to go as heralding a horrible experience. The more he holds on, the harder the retained stool becomes. You are witnessing this vicious cycle when you see him stiffening and becoming red. Unfortunately this memory is subconscious so that he doesn't understand what he needs to do about it. In this situation, my approach is to give a bulk laxative such as lactulose at a dose which is adjusted until the stool is very soft and easy to pass. Over time, provided he continues to pass soft stools regularly, he will forget that it was a painful process and you will be able to reduce and eventually stop the lactulose. This may take up to six months. It is important that your doctor monitors this process as occasionally there are rare conditions that present in this way and your doctor will check for these.

Dr Simon Rowley

habits.

telling fibs

Most children start off being transparently honest. If we walk into the room and the baby is crying and we ask them, 'Who made the baby cry?' they may well announce with pride, 'It was me!'

But as they leave their fourth birthday behind and get closer to their fifth, many of our children turn into competent fibbers.

why children tell fibs

There are many reasons why our children tell fibs. They might be trying to avoid getting into trouble, they might be trying to avoid doing things that they would rather not do, they might be trying to make themselves feel very important or competent, or they might simply be letting their imagination run riot. Most commonly, they are trying to stay out of trouble.

picture the scene

Mum: (having heard the sounds of the pantry door and biscuit jar lid) 'What's that on your hand?'

Child: (hoping to stay out of trouble) 'Nothing.'

Mum: 'But it looks like biscuit.'

Child: (trying to stay out of trouble) 'I don't know.'

Mum: 'What does it taste of?'

Child: 'Yummy.'

Mum: 'Well, I wonder how it got there?'

Child: (last valiant attempt to stay out of trouble) 'I don't know. Maybe a ghost did it.'

Mum is now wondering what on earth she has done to deserve a child who lies. It is likely that she will be cross. The child is no doubt feeling guilty and maybe upset, so how do we avoid these scenes?

don't be the one to tell the first fib

Mum, knowing full well what caused the stuff to be the child's hand, asked, 'What's that on your hand?' and it all went downhill from there. If we want our children to be honest, the first thing we have to do is to model honesty in our own behaviour. It is dishonest to ask our child to confess to something we already know the answer to.

Another example is when we send our children to wash their hands before dinner. They head off in the right direction and return far too soon. We know they have not washed their hands and yet we ask, 'Have you washed your hands properly?'

a better alternative

Mum would have been better off – and far more honest – saying calmly, 'You have been in the biscuit jar. You know that you are not allowed to do that without asking me,' and applied time out.

This way, we have stated the rule and shown our child what happens when 'family rules' are broken. There is no great drama, the point has been made, and our child is not forced into telling fibs.

too much temptation

When a 'family rule' has been broken, it is often a good idea to ask ourselves whether we set up an opportunity that was simply too tempting. Could we have avoided the situation by having the biscuits on a high shelf rather than in easy

Children sometimes tell fibs to get out of doing things that they don't want to do. But it usually starts with us telling the first fib!

Some children tell fibs to show how important they are. If this happens your child needs reassurance from you. Tell you child how proud you are of them.

reach in a see-through glass jar? Was our child alone in the kitchen for longer than she could handle without getting into trouble?

getting out of doing things

Children sometimes tell fibs to get out of doing things that they don't want to do. Again, avoid starting with a fib. Start with making sure they understand why the task at hand has to be done, then continue follow through.

vigilance helps

Vigilance is a very useful parental attribute. If we think our child is not doing as we have asked we should follow up quietly and watch. Appearing at the right moment saves a lot of interrogating and resultant fibbing.

If we think our child is sneakily hurting the baby or taunting the toddler, we can avoid asking, 'What happened?' and getting, 'Nothing', or a tall tale, by simply appearing at the exact moment our child is doing something wrong.

It is all part of getting our children to believe that parents have eyes in the back of their head and wrongdoers will get caught.

admire honesty

When your child does something wrong and tells you about it, let her know that you are proud of her honesty. Rather than punishing the action – which encourages her to fib about wrongdoing – ask her, or discuss with her, what she could do to put it right. Ask her what help she needs from you to follow through on her ideas.

making yourself important

Another way in which our children tell fibs is by making themselves the best, the fastest, the hero or the winner. They

how much you think that she is wonderful. She needs to know that the most important thing to you is that she takes part, that she enjoys the process and that you love to hear about what she did. It is also reasonable to let her know that, while you love to hear about her day, you are not interested in hearing about things that didn't happen.

flights of imagination

Some children love to tell exciting stories. Either through their transparency or through our vigilance, we should be able to work out if a story is just a flight of imagination.

By entering their fantasy, by asking what happened next, by wondering just how fast a green dragon with pink wings could fly across the kindy roof, we make it clear that we know it is a make-believe story.

maybe it is true

When our son was four, he made a new friend at kindy whom he insisted kept tigers at the bottom of his garden. We strenuously denied that this was possible and gave many a lecture to our son on the value of honesty and our horror at the thought of him telling fibs.

The first time we arranged for our son to go and play at his friend's house, we discovered that his father was the Director of the Auckland Zoo!

Diane Levy, Family Therapist

come home and tell us how they built the tallest tower, swung highest in the swing, kicked the ball the furtherest. This happens when our children wish that they were more competent than they are. Again, if you suspect that this is going on, don't interrogate and accuse. Find out the truth of the situation from a reliable adult. Tell your child calmly, 'You told me that you came first in a race yesterday. There was no race yesterday.'

This is a good opportunity to tell your child how proud you are of her, how much you love her and

burping, nose picking & other obsessions

Mum has prepared a delicious meal and the whole family is sitting together for what she hopes will be a pleasant experience. As soon as she sits down, one child burps and giggles! The next child copies, then adds insincerely, 'Pardon me', and bursts into laughter.

The more Mum and Dad growl, the more they burp and giggle. What was meant to be a nice family atmosphere has, once again, turned into a battlefield.

There seems to be a whole lot of childish behaviours that we don't like to talk about, think about, or generally see our children do – and the behaviours aren't necessarily limited to just children! Accompanied by gales of childish laughter, it might seem burping, passing wind, pulling faces, nose picking and rude words are relatively harmless. That is until it happens in front of your elderly neighbour who you know already regards the younger generation as lacking any respect – especially your children! Left unchecked, these behaviours can eventually become deliberately done and ultimately lead on to a deterioration in general behaviour.

Nose picking (and eating it too!) and putting hands down pants are behaviours that feel good to kids but are generally seen as socially unacceptable. There is also swearing, poking out of tongues and rude backchat, which seem to be the particular delight of four year old boys and girls. So how should we best deal with these habits?

swearing and tongue poking

The problem is the first time our children come out with some forbidden Anglo-Saxon term, we get such a shock, we ask, 'What did you say?' So our child co-operates and repeats the offending words.

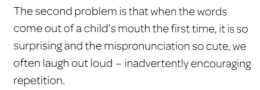

The second problem is that when the words come out of a child's mouth the first time, it is so surprising and the mispronunciation so cute, we often laugh out loud – inadvertently encouraging repetition.

The third problem is the standard advice to, 'Ignore it and it will go away.' This advice has no other effect than to encourage the child to repeat what he has said louder and clearer because, obviously, if we are ignoring his splendid offering, it can only be because we haven't heard him the first time.

And the fourth problem is that our reprimand is likely to be met with, 'But Dad (or Mum) says it!'

Swearing and poking out of tongues come in two forms, needing two different approaches. When the behaviour is aimed directly at us, designed to be offensive and simply meaning, 'Up yours!', we should respond as we would to hitting, biting, spitting or any other unacceptable behaviour. Lead the offender to a suitable time out spot, say very firmly, 'You know you don't do that/speak to me like that,' and add, 'I'll be back to see if you are ready to be respectful.'

When you return, you will know by your child's attitude whether or not he is ready to rejoin the family. If he is calm and apologetic, he is ready. If he is cheeky or giggly, he is not, so tell him, 'You are not ready. I'll pop back in a little while longer,' and don't go back until he has settled down. However, when the swearing or tongue poking is just childish but unacceptable rudeness, give one warning, 'Stop that now!' and pause for your child to settle down.

If he doesn't settle, use time out.

busy hands

Nose picking and hands down the pants are behaviours that are natural but for some people are socially unacceptable.

We are more than a century on from the Victorian horror of anything to do with 'down there' and we can also stop more recent politically correct over-compensating with speeches about, 'It's your body, it's great you feel good about, so it is okay to go and do that in your bedroom.'

But when nose picking and hands down the pants become an obsession,

we need to support our child to control his hand's behaviour. It is okay to remove our child's hand from their nose or pants and say, 'That's not nice, please stop it', and lead them off to another absorbing activity or at least to wash their hands. If the child stops co-operatively and accepts distraction, that's all that is needed.

If he is doing it over and over again, and he's not making any effort to stop the behaviour, put him in time out for two or three minutes. Continue to use time out for as many times as is necessary for him

to learn it is unacceptable behaviour – he'll usually get the idea by about 10 times.

burping and passing wind

Of course burping and passing wind are natural body reactions too, and our first step is to teach our children to say, 'Excuse me' or 'Pardon me', when they are accidental. There also comes a time when our children turn them into a repetitive art form, often accompanied by, 'Excuse me', and followed by hilarious giggling. This is when you will need to conceal your own amusement because by this time, we are 'beyond accidental' and into 'delightedly deliberate'.

Should our child find it necessary to continue after being asked once to stop, it's time for him to go outside or into another room to continue his prowess alone. When he has it out of his system (s'cuse the pun!), he is welcome to return to the family.

mum, dad, stop whining

When you are dealing with nasty habits, it is really important to avoid whining at your child. If you hear yourself saying, 'If I've told you once, I've told you a thousand times . . .', you know the childish behaviour has crossed over from 'one of those things that children do' to 'behaviour that needs to be stopped'. Be aware you are behaving as if whining at your child will change his behaviour. For most of us, this is the triumph of hope over experience.

If there is behaviour we don't like, the first step is to recognise we are whining rather than being proactive. We need to decide for ourselves what we are going to do, in order to let our children know clearly what the rules are, and to behave that way every time the offensive behaviour occurs. If the behaviour is happening in front of you or within earshot, you need to do something about it.

Diane Levy, Family Therapist

If your child is sitting on a swing happily crooning away a series of words you would rather not hear, or you spy him at the end of the garden exploring his nose so deeply you fear for the contents of his brain . . . these are private moments. Creep away without making a sound and try to blot the image out of your mind!

common sense advice from other mums who have had to deter a habit

passing wind at the table

Whenever my four year old farts, usually at the dinner table and followed by roars of laughter, we first ask him to say 'Pardon me'. If he continues, we take him to the toilet and ask him to stay there until he is ready to return to the table without farting.

tongue poking

If my children poke their tongues out, I tell them they might swallow a fly, or worse, a bee. This usually closes their mouths pretty quickly!

burping

My son and his cousin (both four) like burping at each other. It's disgusting and they lead each other on. We give them one chance to stop and if they continue, we turn our backs and ignore them, giving attention to their younger siblings by having lots of noisy fun. The boys soon stop because no-one is looking at or responding to them.

fingernail biting

My daughter bites her nails until they bleed when she's tired. We couldn't get her to stop so we got an adult friend over who bites her nails. She told my daughter she wears a horrible tasting nail paint to stop her biting and offered her some. My daughter didn't like the sound of that and after a few weeks, she stopped biting. When we do catch her every now and then, we ask her if she wants the nail paint!

nose picking

My three year old daughter not only picks her nose, but then eats it! It's embarrassing, especially if visitors are over. So we showed her how to blow her nose using a tissue, then bought her a box of colourful tissues and let her decorate the tissue box. Now she walks around with her tissue box under her arm, blowing her nose whether it needs it or not – at least there's no more nose picking!

hands down pants

Our son regularly put his hands down his pants, often without realising it. Whenever we were out in public, we showed him that other people weren't walking around with their hands down their pants because they are 'private' places. Eventually he got the idea, and it took a few 'rewards' and stickers for every day he managed to keep his pants hand-free.

farters and burpers

We have constant 'farters' and 'burpers' in our house so we've created a 'private place' in our laundry where they can go and do their business alone. Works a treat!

swearing

When our little one blurts out a swear word, we ignore it and her dad immediately makes up a ridiculously long and hard-to-pronounce nonsense word. She thinks it's hilarious, especially when he gets her to repeat the word over and over again, by which time she completely forgets about the swear word.

toenail picker

Our son would pick his toenails at the table. I nagged constantly at him to stop but it just created a huge power struggle, and kept the habit alive and kicking. So we let him choose his behaviour – pick his toenails in the bathroom (and no dinner) or sit at the table and eat dinner. He stopped doing it after about a week.

where's blankie? comfort objects

'Oh no, where's Snuggles. I can't find him. I want Snuggles.'
'Where's my blankie, I can't sleep without blankie?'
'I don't want that cup, I want my green one with the frog on it!'

Does this sound familiar? Just as we get pleasure from our favourite things, so do young children – and they too don't like to have them taken away!

As very young children begin to assert themselves, they will often start making demands. Some of these demands will be reasonable, but with their limited understanding of the world or of what's going on for others, often their demands can seem unrealistic. Around the same time, young children will also often develop a preference for a favourite object they do not like to part with.

Here are some suggestions for dealing with little ones who have a preference for particular objects of comfort.

As your baby grows into a toddler, she is learning more about herself and her environment. She is becoming clear about what she likes and dislikes,

and so she begins demanding to have things a certain way. She declares her independence and clearly disagrees with you by asserting herself and stating, 'No!'

It is essential to give your child the message that her needs are important but at the same time encouraging her to consider others. Your aim should be to teach your child to assert herself while helping her to learn to cope when things don't go her way. You can do this by letting her have what she likes, as long as you are happy with it and it is within reason. But if you run out of her favourite biscuits for example, you needn't go running to the shop because she demands them.

Also, don't give in when you feel it's not justified or you have good reason why you don't want to, for example, drive all the way home again because you have left her favourite doll behind. Instead, acknowledge your child's wishes, ('I know you want me to go back home to pick up your doll to take to playgroup . . .'), while letting her know the reason she can't have her way ('. . . but there is no time for that now or we will be late and miss out on sing-time and morning tea.') If possible, offer her an alternative, ('Today let's play with the dolls at playgroup').

Most young children will become attached to some form of comfort object, whether it's a blanket, doll or soft toy. This often begins between 8–12 months of age. These special objects are referred to as transitional objects because of children associating them with Mum or Dad and even using them to take their parents place to make separations more manageable.

On the one hand, comfort objects can be very beneficial for providing emotional and tangible comfort in times of need – they can help children to relax and fall asleep when they are tired, to feel better when they are sad, to help settle them in new and unfamiliar situations or environments such as a new childcare, and to feel secure when Mum or Dad are not there. On the other hand, children can sometimes be so head-over-heels in love with their comfort object that it becomes a nightmare for parents.

When dealing with a child who has a comfort object, allow her to have it within reason. Consider her need for it in unsettling times while at the same time bearing in mind that you don't have to give in to her every whim.

If your child is unable to take her special object to preschool or kindy, offer a substitute. She could

Children become very attached to their comfort object and it is important never to tease them about it.

instead have a photo of you, a piece of her blankie to hide in her trouser pocket or a 'picture' note from you to keep in her bag or lunchbox.

Never force your child to give up her comfort object. Forcing her to give it up is only going to upset her. Your child will outgrow it on her own and in her own time. Being emotionally available to your child will help her to continue to develop her sense of security so that one day she will no longer need her favourite object.

points to consider

- Never tease your child about her comfort object. And don't let others tease her either.
- When she's crying, comfort her before offering her comfort object.
- If her comforter is dirty, wash it when she's busy or asleep to avoid her getting upset.
- Buy a replica or two so if you lose or need to wash a cherished item you have a spare.
- Limit her use by allowing it only at certain times (bedtime) or places (bedroom).
- If she has forgotten her comforter distract her by playing a game or show her something so her mind, and hands, are kept busy.
- Don't take it off her if it's a busy or stressful time in your lives, i.e. a new baby, starting preschool or going through a separation.

Chantal Gazal, Registered Psychologist

nervous blinking

Q: My son suddenly developed a nervous blinking of his eyes not long after starting school. We took him to an optometrist who gave him the all clear and while the habit stopped for a while, it has returned and seems to be more like a 'tic' – one eye twitches as well as the whole side of his face and it is very prominent. I've been told it is probably a nervous 'quirk' rather than a visual problem. He only does it a few times a day, but it happens at times when we wouldn't expect him to be nervous, such as when he's playing. He isn't aware he is doing it. I'd love some information about the cause and treatment as it seems to be a very common thing that children develop but information is hard to find. I'm concerned my son's 'quirk' will soon become apparent to other children and he could be ridiculed, leading to his condition becoming worse.

A: You are describing what is known as a 'tic', a repetitive involuntary movement that can occur up to hundreds of times a day and is most commonly a facial twitching or grimace. The most frequent types of tics are eye blinking or sniffing. Sometimes a tic will disappear only to return in a different form, as has happened with your son. Tics are thought to occur commonly in as many as 20 per cent of all children. They're also more common in boys than girls, and children are usually of school age. Tics are generally harmless, although sometimes they will accompany speech (Tourette's syndrome) and this occurrence tends to be more serious and persistent. There is no 'cure' and it is thought the best thing to do is to ignore the presence of the tic, as paying too much attention to it may actually make it worse. They tend to occur more often in times of stress but as you may have noticed with your son, they can in fact occur at any time. Most will eventually disappear within a few months or a year, and sometimes medication is used with varying success to try and hasten their disappearance.

Dr Simon Rowley

rude words

Q: My nearly four year old boy thinks it is funny to say, 'Poo' and, 'Bum'. We have been telling him we don't say those words and putting him in his room, but when you're in the car on the motorway, it's a bit difficult to put him in his room! Should we ignore the behaviour or address it? And really, is this just a boy thing? There is so much conflicting information around about four year olds using rude words – jump on it now, it's just a phase, if you ignore it will it go away, if you don't do something he will just keep on, it's a boy thing, it's a four year old thing – that it is hard to know which way a parent should jump.

A: I am sure your son knows the words he is using are unacceptable and he knows how to use them at a time when you are least able to act. Therefore, I am going to recommend action rather than ignoring or waiting for it to go away. At home, beef up your disapproval. When he uses those words, scoop him off to his room and say very strongly, 'You know that we don't use those words around here.' When he uses them in the car, say very strongly, 'You know that we don't use those words. That will be time out.' You be the time out. Don't talk to him until you get home. Then pop him in his room and unpack the car slowly.

Diane Levy

clearing her throat

Q: My four-year-old daughter constantly clears her throat. It seems to be worse in the mornings and evenings, but she can go all day clearing her throat every few seconds. In the past she has had a constant cough which was successfully treated with asthma medications, but after about seven months we stopped using them. Then a few months later she started clearing her throat again. She doesn't have a cold or sore throat but had tonsillitis earlier this year. She restarted the asthma medications two months ago without success. She is also half way through a 10-day course of steroids with little, if any, success. She once had a significant allergic reaction but we don't know what it was in reaction to. After skin and blood tests, I was told she has only mild allergies to dairy, wheat and eggs and we should not bother avoiding them. She also has mild eczema. Could the throat clearing be an allergy? How do we find out? And if it's not that, what else could it be?

A: It is unlikely this throat clearing is due to any medical problem, particularly as possible causes, such as asthma, allergy and chronic nasal infection, appear to have been considered and ruled out. This symptom is a bit more likely to represent a habit which has become ingrained and your daughter is unaware or unconscious to the fact she is doing it. Sometimes we call these little habits 'tics'. They often start for a valid reason, such as a cold with a subsequent irritable cough, but then the child continues to do it even after the irritant phase of the cold has long disappeared. Similarly eye-blinking tics often start after conjunctivitis. The best thing to do is to ignore it and eventually it will disappear. Allergy may cause excessive phlegm and cough but this is unlikely to be the cause here, particularly if there are no other symptoms of allergy such as itchy eyes, skin problems or obvious food reactions.

Dr Simon Rowley

pulling out hair

Q: My daughter is 20 months old and for the last two months she has been pulling out her hair – mainly in the evenings and overnight. It has got to the stage where she is developing a bald spot on top of her head! We have tried using distractions with toys but she still does it. A new sister arrived in the last month and we thought this might be contributing to it. However, the behaviour started before her sister was born.

A: I am assuming that your little girl has invented this behaviour as her own response to when she feels uncomfortable, frustrated or a bit anxious. I would recommend offering a cuddle each time she looks as if she might begin pulling her hair or when she actually does it. Don't comment on her hair-pulling. Just say, 'You look like a girl who needs a cuddle.' Scoop her up in your arms and hold her gently and without further comment until she wriggles to get down. I am confident that supporting her emotions (worry, frustration, upset, anxiety) in this way, without trying to take the emotions away by distracting her, will enable her to get over the feeling and carry on with some other activity.

Diane Levy

finger sucking

Q: I would appreciate advice to help stop my six year old son from sucking his fingers. He has sucked his fingers since he was about four months old and generally only sucks them for comfort or when he is tired and sleepy. He sucks his middle and index fingers. Now that his baby teeth have gone and are about to be replaced by new adult teeth, I would really like this sucking to stop as I fear for the new teeth – and a huge dentist bill in years to come! I have tried smothering his fingers with the foul tasting clear liquid, and wrapping his fingers in tape and bandages, but without success.

A: Finger and thumb sucking is a harmless and normal form of comfort or security for a child. Babies have been observed on ultrasound scans to be finger or thumb sucking inside the womb, and occasionally are born with sucking blisters on their hands. Most children will stop the habit of their own accord between the ages of two and four, and any later, peer pressure at school usually puts an end to it as other children point out the babyish nature of the action. Although there is a lot of public concern about what finger or thumb sucking does to emerging teeth, there is no good evidence that it is responsible for irreversible dental malocclusion or similar problems in the first few years. However, once the second teeth begin to emerge (around seven years of age), there is more concern. Usually for any deforming force to have such an impact it would need to be exerted 24 hours a day with sustained pressure, i.e. braces. The best approach is to ignore it or to offer a gentle distraction as it enables your child to take up another activity with their hands without necessarily drawing attention to it. A child of six or seven years is perfectly capable of having a discussion about the problem and may be encouraged to make his own suggestion about the best strategy. As frustrating as it can be, you will need to be patient and confident that the finger sucking habit will eventually stop. Your dentist may also be able to assess the situation and offer further advice.

Dr Simon Rowley

scratching and scars

Q: My child is two and a half and sucks her thumb, which doesn't really bother me, but at the same time, she scratches her face. She has been doing it for about a year and has scratched so much, it is beginning to scar. We've tried everything. We've been to the doctor and tried a number of creams (some very expensive ones). We've tried to stop her from sucking her thumb, we've taped socks on her hands at night but she takes them off, and even covering the scratched spot with plasters and tapes but she pulls this off too. We keep her nails very short but she still can't stop scratching. She has just started kindy and we're worried about infection and the chance of permanent scarring to her lovely face.

A: Although it is worrying to see your child scratching her face, there is really very little risk that permanent scarring will occur. The tissues in this area are well supplied with blood vessels and heal very well. Obviously it is important to try hard to keep her nails short and clean so as to minimise the risk of infection. In fact, the best way to accelerate the disappearance of the habit is to ignore it. The more negative attention the child gets, the more she is likely to continue it. A good idea is to distract her quietly when you see her scratching by offering something else to do with her hands.

Dr Simon Rowley

naked obsession

Q: I have two sons aged seven and three. They both enjoy being naked! I constantly find the seven year old dancing naked in front of the full length mirror and, whenever possible they are naked out in the garden (they even apply their own sunscreen!) Whilst this doesn't bother me too much, I am wondering whether it is time to have a little chat with the seven year old. My husband and I don't hide ourselves, the boys have seen us in the shower, on the toilet and dressing and I understand that they find their bodies quite normal. However, is it time perhaps to let the older one know that, 'Schoolboys don't go without their underpants when they are playing,' or something to that effect? I suppose that foolishly I am worried about what other people think.

A: One of the most useful phrases, I taught my children, very early on was, 'That's not appropriate.' This was useful to cover a whole lot of behaviour that, while there was nothing terribly wrong with it, made me or other people feel uncomfortable. Your phrase, 'Whilst this doesn't bother me too much,' indicates that it is bothering you. If it is making you feel uncomfortable, then that is a good clue that there is something about the way your seven year old is dancing around that is probably inappropriate. Many of our norms of behaviour are set by unspoken agreement and so it is not foolish to worry about what other people think. Our children need to feel good about their bodies but they also need to be taught suitable modesty.

Diane Levy

advice from mums who have successfully deterred thumb sucking & pacifiers

cut the tip off

My son had a 'dummy' until he was about two years old. He kept it under his pillow at night. On the advice of a friend, I cut the tip off the nipple of his dummy and told him that it was broken. When he tried sucking it, it didn't feel right. Then when I offered it to him at night, he didn't want it. I kept a whole one in the drawer 'just in case', but he never asked for it. No dramas, no crying – it was so simple.

purposely lost

My son had his beloved pacifier since day one, and wouldn't leave home without one. When he was around two years old, I decided it was time to live without it (actually all four of them). One day when he couldn't find his pacifier, I told him that 'he' had lost it and Mummy didn't know where it was. Together we looked everywhere but couldn't find it (of course because Mummy had made sure it couldn't be found). Surprisingly it worked! He really believed I didn't know where it was and that he had lost it so he wasn't screaming at me asking for it. Although the first night without it was a little rocky and I felt a little guilty, we got through it.

all wrapped up

We asked our son if we could give his dummy to his best friend's new baby brother. He agreed to this, and now when he asks for it, we remind him it's all wrapped up for the new baby. To stop thumb sucking, my mother used to say to me (I was a thumb sucker), 'You must be tired because you're sucking your thumb. I think you need a nap.' Apparently I whipped my thumb out of my mouth so fast, and after a couple of weeks, I stopped sucking my thumb altogether.

fairy exchange

Both of my children (now aged three and two years) had a pacifier or 'bub bub' as they called it. To get rid of the pacifier we invented a 'bub bub' fairy. After their second birthday, we told them the fairy had to take their 'bub bub' to another little baby who needed it. The children put it in the letterbox so the fairy could collect it overnight. In its place, the fairy would leave them a present. Worked a treat!

plaster it up

A tested method in our family to stop thumb sucking, which has been used on several generations of children, is to coat the offending thumbs with a bitter-tasting paint (for deterring nail biters) which you get from the chemist. Additionally for bed when an awful taste alone may not be enough, wrap the thumb in fabric sticking plaster which also makes it uncomfortable to suck thumb while sleeping.

stop and grow

My daughter started thumb sucking around 10 weeks old, and as she got older, the more she sucked it. By the time she was three years old, her thumb was extremely red and raw. I painted a nail biting solution onto her nail and we talked about the horrible taste and the fact that it would help her stop sucking. During the day it was a breeze, but at night she would wake and start gagging on the taste of her thumb. We persevered and every couple of days I painted more on her thumbnail. After three nights, she broke the habit and got a special doll for being so clever. Now, at four years old she is a happy contented little girl.

throwing away ceremony

When my son turned two, I felt it was time to wean him off his pacifier, or better still, get rid of it altogether. He had used it since he was three weeks old and it definitely soothed him. So I cut the teat in half and, of course, as soon as he popped it into his mouth, it fell out. After another couple of attempts, he brought it over to me looking mystified. I explained it was broken, probably because he was a big boy of two, and I couldn't repair it. We held a small ceremony to 'throw it away' and after just one night of him wanting it, we never looked back. Now at four and a half, we just need to get rid of the blankie!

playing.

playing fair

Young children don't naturally know how to share. Rather it's a development skill that gradually builds and develops as children get older and experience new and different things. Therefore, it's up to us, as parents, to help them learn.

Two-year-old Clare is rummaging through her toy box and comes across her younger brother Ben's musical keyboard tucked at the bottom. Excited, she pulls it out and starts to play. It's not long before four-year-old Ben comes hurtling towards her, shouting, "No, that's mine!" Clare shouts back, 'No, mine!'

Ben: 'Give it back…'

Clare: 'No!'

A tug-of-war ensues.

Sound familiar? Clare and Ben aren't intentionally being nasty and selfish towards each other. They're still learning the art of fair play and how to share their things.

During the toddler and preschool years, there are three main developmental stages children will go through. Depending on what stage your child is at, will determine her ability to play and share with others.

18 months – 3 years

Sharing is beyond these developmentally young littlies. Toddlers are only beginning to understand the concept of ownership and that something can be theirs. As babies they happily give up anything they are holding with little concern or worry. But as they develop into toddlers, they begin to develop a sense of identity and possessions start to become extremely important to them.

Toddlers begin to feel so attached to their toys, that if you take one away it can feel as if you're taking away a part of them. This is why toddlers often use the expression, 'Mine!' Toddlers are notorious for claiming to own objects that aren't even theirs. You can help them to learn about ownership by talking about what's theirs and what's not: These are Mummy's shoes and these are your shoes.'

The concept of time is also often beyond them, making the idea of taking turns and sharing difficult for them to grasp. Having to wait, even if for a few seconds, for their turn to play with a toy, or to go on the swing, can be too much for them to handle. What's going on right now matters more to them than what is going to happen in the next five minutes. It's hardly surprising then, that a two year old doesn't understand why he should wait for another child to finish playing with a toy before he can have a turn – or why he should stop playing with something just to let someone else have a turn.

It takes time and practice for toddlers to develop an understanding of time and to accept waiting to have a go. Rather than trying to force toddlers to share, which doesn't teach them anything, focus on repetition and let them practise sharing with others who know how to share, like an older sibling or adult,

and show them how: 'I'll have a go throwing the ball and then it's your turn to throw the ball.'

When there is a dispute, distraction is useful, especially given a toddler's short attention span. Often by moving the focus of their concentration from one object to another, any dispute is resolved.

During this stage, young children also begin to learn that others do sometimes think and feel differently to the way they do, and that what they might like others won't. When your toddler is playing side by side with another child, be ready to intervene. With

remember

- Demonstrate sharing by example.

- Praise or encourage them when they share willingly.

- Don't call children 'selfish' or punish them for not sharing.

- Don't expect them to share everything; set aside a few items that are okay not to share.

- Don't expect too much, too early - sharing is learned but it will come.

their limited language abilities, toddlers are often unable to express exactly what they want and may resort to grabbing and pulling. Their tolerance is also limited and they quickly become frustrated, so an aggressive response can often follow, such as hitting or biting. The best way to deal with this is to re-direct them to something else, or remove them for some time out.

3-4 years

Developing empathy makes sharing easier. During this stage a child's ability to share increases dramatically as they develop two important skills. The first is empathy, the ability to understand another person's needs, feelings or perspective. A child may see and understand that another child wants something they have and they decide to give them the toy to make them happy.

The second is the development of language skills so they can better handle frustrations. Rather than resorting to grabbing, crying or shouting, children begin to verbalise what they want.

They also begin to better understand the concept of time. However, this skill is still limited and they will still need your help to learn to be patient and to take turns. For example, if they are doing a puzzle or playing with a particular toy, setting a timer for 5 or 10 minutes can be a useful strategy because it clearly shows (and sounds) how long they have to wait.

Sharing comes more easily in environments where objects or possessions do not belong to them,

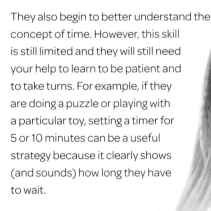

such as early childcare centres, playgroups, etc. To encourage sharing at home between siblings, look to provide toys and activities that encourage co-operative play, such as dress-ups, building and construction toys, games with more than one player, arts and crafts, etc.

If your child has a friend over to play, discuss with her in advance which treasured toys she doesn't want to share and put them away. Then gently remind her about the rules for sharing.

As young children become better at sharing, teach them to work out their own deals. For example, 'If you both want to play with the truck, what can you do?' See if they can come up with a plan without you. If not, make a suggestion and ask for their

opinion. 'Ben, why don't you play with the big truck for 10 minutes now, and Clare, you can play with the cars until 10 minutes are up? Or do you have another suggestion?' It will take some practice before young children can make deals on their own but, with your help, they can begin to work towards this skill which will be invaluable for years to come.

4-5 years

Preschoolers love to play together and friendship becomes much more important to them at this stage. They come to realise that sharing has its benefits, mostly because it's more fun playing with others than it is to play alone.

Around this age, they also come to understand that generosity is important in developing and maintaining friendships. 'If I play with this on my own, Jamie will be bored and want to go home', so they become more motivated to work out sharing solutions. They also understand consequences - if they share with their friend now, their friend will share with them later.

Naturally, we want our children to get along with others – to share, to be considerate and to be caring around friends - and while we can teach them many of these skills, sometimes we should also stand back and let other children show them how – children learn best by doing.

Reassuringly, as children get older they soon work out the many benefits of sharing – mostly that play takes on a whole new level of fun if everyone is included!

Chantal Gazal, Registered Psychologist

imaginary friends

Has an imaginary playmate suddenly appeared in your family? Don't be alarmed, it's perfectly normal during the preschool years. Whether your child's friend is the sort to pop in occasionally for a visit or if they are ever-present, imaginary friends are in most cases an extension of pretend play created by a child's imagination.

Most are invisible playmates or they can be inspired by an animal or favourite toy. Some children will create just one, while others invent a whole family! Imaginary friends usually appear on the scene between the ages of three and four and are slightly more common with the firstborn and only-child as well as for children with siblings who are far apart in age. This may be because they spend more time alone and have more privacy than a group of closely spaced siblings.

more common in girls

Girls are more likely to have imaginary friends than boys. Boys tend to do more impersonations of characters than interacting with imaginary people.

the ideal companion

Imaginary friends offer many advantages for young children. They are the ideal companion – they are always available and willing to play, are co-operative, like their creators' ideas and games, and never hog favourite toys! They can be a protector (to save them from the 'monster' under the bed), someone to keep them company, or a positive coping tool to help deal with times of stress or change, such as moving house, a new baby, or starting a new kindy or daycare. An imaginary friend provides an outlet for children to express and work through the everyday anxieties of growing up and learning to make sense of the big wide world.

Often invisible friends will disappear of their own accord when a child no longer has a 'need' for them. The only cause for concern would be if your child prefers to play exclusively with their invisible playmate and avoids meaningful interactions with other children.

Watch and listen to your child's interactions with their imaginary friend. If they are comfortable with their interest, you might ask a few questions, but let your child guide you. They'll tell you what they want you to know.

your involvement

When adults get too involved, children may feel they've lost control of their creation – which defeats the purpose! So be aware of entering your child's imaginary world too enthusiastically or interacting with an imaginary friend without being invited.

Keep your ears open. Discreetly eavesdropping on interactions between your child and companion may open a window into your child's world, giving you insight into their current challenges.

It is common for children to have an imaginary friend. A make-believe play friend or animal can be good for children with a fertile imagination offering a constant source of companionship and comfort.

Sometimes an imaginary friend can help parents to see where a problem is.

Try to be accommodating with imaginary friends, but if requests are unreasonable, feel free to set limits. If your child wants, for example, a place set at the dinner table for the imaginary pal but you have guests over and there's no space, it's okay to say, 'There's no room tonight. I think Robin will have to sit somewhere else while we eat.'

Sometimes children project their own thoughts and feelings onto their 'invisible' companions. If your child tells you the imaginary friend gets a sore tummy when the lights are turned out for bedtime, listen to the message behind the words.

Imaginary friends can also be convenient scapegoats. Young children tend to measure mishaps based on damage rather than intention. Accidentally knocking over a glass of milk may seem as bad to them as purposefully throwing it on the floor since the result is the same – a mess! If your child blames mishaps on the imaginary friend, it could be there is a fear of consequences far worse than you think the situation merits. Keep reminding your child of your love no matter what has been done and that it's okay to have accidents – the blame game should soon disappear!

While young children do sometimes blur the lines between

fantasy and reality, most know their imaginary pal is pretend. But if you really don't feel comfortable playing along with them, you can still respond positively without stifling creativity by saying, 'I love your imagination when you play with your friend.'

Imagination plays a key role in children's abilities to think creatively and adapt to different situations. Support and encourage this through everyday experiences and activities and through your own creativity.

Expose your child to a wide variety of real life experiences that inspire. Visit art galleries, libraries, parks and recreation centres. Talk about the people you meet in everyday life such as the doctor, police officer, librarian and shop attendant and discuss what roles they play.

Share lots of different books with your child. Seek out the classics as well as modern fantasy stories that allow children to think about non-reality.

Provide time and props for pretend play experiences – and join in when you are invited.

If you are comfortable with your own imagination, introduce an imaginary friend or pet of your own. Try a small bird cupped in the palm of your hand.

Make up a story – has it fallen out of its nest and lost its mother? Take turns holding and stroking the bird. Talk about how soft it feels and how frightened it must be. Maybe you could go for a walk and 'find' the tree it fell out of, leaving it at the bottom of the tree for its mother to find?

So if your child's imaginary friend, whether it be just one, two or a whole family of friends, come knocking on your door, welcome them in and then join in the fun of your child's vivid imagination!

Dianne Krissansen, Early Childcare Educator

war, guns & violent play

How come we calm, non-aggressive, peace-loving parents manage to acquire high-energy, rampaging preschoolers who seem determined to race around yelling, waving weapons and taking aim?

Some of us may have been determined there would be no war play, battle scenes and definitely no weaponry of any sort, only to be startled by our preschooler dashing into the kitchen pointing his first two fingers in a trigger-like fashion and yelling, 'Bang! You're dead, Mummy!' Is it inevitable? Is it part of 'boys will be boys'? Should we be stopping it? Do we have a responsibility to prevent it?

Our children, both girls and boys, need to do a lot of running around, climbing, shouting and social play. Most play is not totally unstructured and even though we may set up completely free play, i.e. giving our children access to all sorts of toys and equipment without making any suggestions, our children inevitably start adding in their own structure and rules.

Think about it. Even if you give your child a box of pegs and a board with 100 holes, once they are past the stage where putting the peg in the hole is the activity, they start to create rows or blocks of colours and set out the pegs in some sort of pattern. In other words, we are driven to make some sort of order out of what is apparently random, to make what we do become directional and purposeful.

Similarly when our children get together in groups, they rarely spend the time running around in circles. In fact, if they are aimlessly running around in circles with no plan or structure, we can be pretty sure the situation will rev up and get out of hand and we should introduce some sort of structure before trouble breaks out.

what's good about it?

So one good thing about war play is children are developing rules and structure to their play, often involving 'your side/my side', sticking to some rules of play, and developing a sense of a game having a start and finish point.

When they rush in and point something, and say, 'Bang! You're dead!' they are not talking about maiming or killing a friend, they are usually indicating there is a mutual agreement in the game that the 'dead' person will lie down on the ground for a while, get up whole and healthy and do it all over again. They are learning about rules, fair play and co-operation.

The joy of make-believe where you can put on a red cape and fly through the air and save good people from bad people is one of the joys of childhood and part of the delightful development of fantasy and imaginative play.

can't they learn those things some other way?

Of course they can. They can learn about rules of behaviour by us teaching them not to hit people, annoy people, hurt people, snatch things or use unkind and nasty words. They can also learn the rules of fair play – taking turns, winning or taking defeat graciously, helping those less competent by giving them an advantage – when we play board games or card games together, when we show them the rules and skills of various outdoor games, when we take them to a playground and watch

The joy of make-believe where you can put on a red cape and fly through the air and save good people from bad people is one of the joys of childhood and part of the delightful development of fantasy and imaginative play.

The reasons to allow or not allow war toys and war games are complex and far-reaching and not within the realms of a three or four year old to grasp.

them take risks, take care and take turns.

why war games and weapons

I need to confess that I have absolutely no idea. I can see no merit or excitement in these games (whether real life, pretend or electronic) and have never had a desire to play them – whether as a child, as a parent or as an adult.

However, my girl and boy children, many of my friend's children and many of my adult friends take great delight in these sorts of games, yet tend to be the same people who weep over a story about a neglected puppy, are averse to killing spiders and love watching hideous war movies.

So I retreat to saying, 'I don't know', but it seems to give many people lots of pleasure and there seems to be little connection between the fantasy world and the real-world actions of socially well-adjusted people.

what do adults fear?

We fear our children will become aggressive and lose respect for the sanctity of life. We fear they will find it an easy transition from pointing a plastic water gun to firing a round of bullets into a group of people. We fear by condoning the war play of preschoolers, we are somehow condoning and encouraging violence and lack of respect for the sanctity of human life.

As adults, we understand war and its destruction, and that tragedy and loss is a dreadful thing to be avoided at all costs. We don't need, however, to place our sophisticated and long-term fears and doubts on the shoulders of preschool children.

either allow or don't

The reasons to allow or not allow war toys and war games are complex and far-reaching and not within the realms of a three

or four year old to grasp. So don't expect to stop war play by an explanation supposed to convince your child not to take part in something that looks like great fun.

If you are adamant you don't want your children to have war toys or to play with war toys, feel free to say 'No'. Your children will suffer no deprivation or harm, but be prepared for them to learn to play those sorts of games out of your sight and at other people's places.

Stick to brief phrases like, 'We don't play these sorts of games in our home because they can be unkind and dangerous.' Make sure you are consistent in enforcing the rule.

If you don't see these toys and games as leading to aggression and hostility, feel free to allow them as long as you keep an eye out for fair play and lack of physical aggression over and above the normal rough-and-tumble of childhood.

Ensure all the rules of fair play are upheld – no hitting, tormenting or imprisonments beyond a few minutes. Everyone needs to take turns at being the 'goodie' or 'baddie', the winner or the loser, the invincible and the conquered.

Afternoon tea will be served to all participants at the end of battle.

Diane Levy, Family Therapist

young children & television

There's no denying entertaining preschoolers can sometimes be hard work and with our hectic lifestyles, television for some can be a convenient short-term babysitter as we catch up on housework, make a phone call or prepare dinner. For others, it simply provides time out for relaxation and a breather for all.

It seems, however, that everywhere we turn, there is compelling new evidence of the corrosive effect of the cathode tube. Is it any wonder we worry about television and the impact it has on our children?

In a perfect world, we'd be home all day having wonderful one-on-one with our preschoolers – but in reality, life is crammed full of demands and try as we might, it's just not possible for most. So there are many practical things you can do to manage your child's television viewing habits.

It starts by being aware of how your preschooler interacts with television, and understanding the types of programmes suitable for the stage your child is at. Similar to reading the food labels in the supermarket, by being aware of the different ingredients in television, you can avoid 'buying' into those considered 'unhealthy' for your child.

children assume television is 'real'

Young children don't bring a great deal of background knowledge to the couch and they assume everything they see on TV is a reflection of real life. If something has arms, legs, eyes, and a body, it must exist – somewhere. The more television they watch, the more real they think it is.

Until about six years old, children are not equipped to work out the motives behind the characters actions.

television interaction

These are general age guidelines.

under 2 years

- Think objects on television exist inside the set.
- Believe everything they see without question.
- Cannot distinguish between beginnings and endings – but they can tell the difference between the programme and advertisements only because their favourite characters go away (sometimes they may cry when this happens).
- Very few of the programmes are made specifically for this age group, but the shows that play in the preschool zones are generally safe for them to watch.

Preschoolers think everything on television is real. And the more television they watch, the more real they think it is.

Programmes this age group might like:
Wiggles, Barney, Bananas in Pyjamas, Little Bear

2–3 year olds
- Still see the characters on television as solid objects (for example, if they see a picture of a bowl of fruit they think if the TV was turned upside down it would all spill out).
- Start to differentiate between ad breaks and programmes.
- By two and a half, a child chooses to watch television rather than television attracting their attention from other activities.

Programmes this age group might like:
Blue's Clues, Maisy, Party Animals

3–4 year olds
- Between three and four, there is a huge learning curve as children gain a greater understanding of symbols. They start to realise the characters they see are pictures and not actually little people.
- By about three, they realise they cannot influence events on television.
- By four they know the difference between news, shows for children, and adult programming.

Programmes this age group might like:
Hi–5, Sesame Street, Tractor Tom, Bob the Builder, Clifford, Dress Up Box

4–6 year olds
- You'll see them play-acting more.

They're trying to work out the finer points of what is real and unreal.
- They assume the characters think similarly to them.
- By about six most can differentiate between human, animated, and puppet characters.

Programmes this age might like:
Dora the Explorer, and gentle family shows - The Zoo

when to let them watch

There are advertising-free Preschool Programme Zones (PPZ) on most New Zealand television channels. PPZ programmers place well-researched, educational shows specifically suited for under five year olds in these 'zones'. The following stations allocate these time slots as preschool programme zones:
TV2: Weekdays 8.30–9.30 a.m.
TV3: Weekdays 6.30–7.10 a.m. and 8.30–9 a.m. Saturday morning 6.30–7.30 a.m.
Maori Television: Weekdays 10–11 a.m. (Kohanga Reo preschool slot).

If your child is watching television outside of these zones, they may need monitoring. A programme rated 'G' is generally more suitable for older children rather than preschoolers. If you still wish for your child to watch television, consider an age-appropriate video or DVD instead.

When you next pop your child in front of the television, remember the two mantras: preschoolers think everything they see is real, and they don't understand why characters on television behave like they do. And of course – you could hide the remote and head outside instead!

viewing guidelines

- Watch television with your child – they learn a lot more, particularly if what is onscreen is discussed, even disagreed with.
- Monitor how conflict is resolved – if the hero is rewarded for resolving conflict positively, that's a great message. Verbally disapprove of violence and highlight positive behaviour. Talk about your personal values with your child. You can also use television to show examples of behaviour and values you disagree with.

- Turn the set off once the chosen show ends. Try not to have it on all the time as background noise. Alternatively put your television in a position where it can be shut away, i.e. in a cabinet – out of sight, out of mind!

- Television is not necessarily 'time out' as a child's imagination is highly active. Remember 'the more they watch, the more they're influenced' and the shows with greatest effect are the ones they think are real.

- Make sure television is just one of many leisure activities on offer. Rewarding or withholding it in order to discipline makes it seem even more alluring to a littlie!

- Make sure an adult is near if the news is on. The content is often scary for a child but it can help if you are explaining and reassuring alongside. Watch for signs of anxiety such as sleeplessness, bad dreams, fears, crying or bedwetting as it may be that what your child has seen is the cause.

- Balance each hour viewed with 15 minutes of physical activity and make sure there is time kept spare for this.

Liz Donnelly, Children's Media Specialist

mums & dads.

how not to lose the plot

You discover green crayon scribbled the length of the hallway wall. You're running late and as you head out the door your child announces he's, 'been in the cake tin!' While you reach for a towel your child knocks over a cup of milk all over the floor.

You ask your child for the umpteenth time to pick up their toys and are met with a stubborn, 'No!' Children seem to be at their worst when you're least able to handle it and as your blood begins to boil, before you know it you say something you shouldn't have – and probably wouldn't have if you weren't so harassed!

Some people are born with calm natures but for the majority of us, we have to work at it – especially when it comes to parenting! The challenge is to be able to stop and think clearly in the instant before you 'lose it'. Here are some cooling strategies to help stop your meltdowns before they start and keep you calm when you're feeling frazzled.

in a hurry

You're in a hurry, your child refuses to put on her shoes and you fly off the handle. You're going to be late again!

calm strategy:

Stress magnifies every little problem so before you're about to snap, tell yourself out loud to 'Stop', close your eyes and take a slow deep breath to calm yourself down. Even if you're in a hurry, it's more beneficial to take a few moments to calm down. Go outside and look at the sky or walk to the letterbox and back. When you're feeling composed, go back and explain to your child, 'Mummy got cross because I asked you to put your shoes on and we are in a rush and you went slow.' Then offer them a reasonable alternative. 'Let's get your shoes on fast and then we'll have time to go to the park before we go to the doctor's. If you don't put on your shoes, we won't have time to go to the park on the way to my appointment.'

Your child learns what you model. You can't

expect your child to learn self-control if you don't model it. To avoid blowing up over the smallest of things, make sure your expectations are realistic and age-appropriate for your child. Get up earlier or start preparing your child earlier so you're not always rushing and constantly saying, 'Quickly, we're going to be late.'

on the phone

You're on the phone and your child starts acting up, pulling at your leg and whining.

calm strategy:

As the old adage says, prevention is better than the cure (it's better to prevent it if you can). When you're busy and your concentration is divided, children naturally become more demanding because you're not giving them all the attention they want. Your child may also be too young to understand you're temporarily unavailable because you're talking to someone

To avoid blowing up over the smallest of things, make sure your expectations are realistic and age-appropriate for your child.

177

Recognise what sets you off. Before you blow your top, stop and count to 10 and ask yourself if you really need to flip out over this.

else on the other end of the phone. When he interrupts, say, 'Excuse me' to the person you're talking to so you're modelling how you'd like your child to behave, and then turn to your child and say, 'I'm talking to Grandma on the phone. I'll be busy for five minutes and when I hang up, we'll read a book.' Give him a hug if you can and return to your conversation and make sure you finish in the five minutes if you can. If he's really losing it, you may have to end the phone call. Don't yell or threaten punishment as this will only increase your child's anxiety and make it harder for them to co-operate.

Prevention is the best strategy. If you're planning to be on the phone, set up some activities beforehand for your child to happily do alone but so that you can sit next to them while on the phone – a puzzle, crayons and paper for drawing, picture cards – or put a toy phone on the table for them so they can make a call too. It's a good idea to keep phone calls relatively short around very young ones with short attention spans and save long chats until they're napping or in bed at night. When your child co-operates, show you have noticed: 'You were really quiet and I could finish my call, thanks. Now I can I play.'

tips, spills and other 'messes'

Your child accidentally (or perhaps deliberately) spills her bowl of cereal on the floor, followed by her cup of milk. .

calm strategy: Your child is probably just as upset as you are and likely to be more worried about what they have lost out of their cup than the mess it has created. Before you blow your top, stop and count to 10 (and back again if necessary) and ask yourself if you really want to flip out over this, especially if the spill was unintentional. Calmly clean up the mess, without saying a word if necessary and they'll calm down quicker. Then explain, 'We don't do that with our food or drink at the table – that's for messy play when we're outside.' If you can learn to recognise the difference between a minor

inconvenience and a major disaster, you're less likely to yell and scream.

other 'calming' tools

portable entertainment: Fill a backpack or tote bag with snacks, water, story books, quiet toys (calculators keep little fingers busy!) and spare nappies or underpants, and leave in your car. Diversions can make all the difference to ward off bad behaviour and boredom when you're stuck waiting at the doctor's or get caught in rush-hour traffic on the way home.

recognise what sets you off: A meltdown doesn't usually appear out of nowhere and is usually a slow build up so if you can find out what tests your patience, you can avoid losing it completely: More sleep? Low blood sugar? Hungry? Too frantic? Or do you start shouting? Dropping things? Onset of a headache? That's a signal to cut back on some commitments if you can so that you can really enjoy the commitments you do make instead of feeling rushed all the time. It doesn't matter that you child doesn't go to every party they're invited to, especially if it means you'll be a less stressed and calm parent!

keep a diary: Even when you've had a bad day, write down something good that has happened or that you're thankful for. This helps to keep a positive perspective so that the next time you become frustrated, you can more easily turn a difficult situation into a positive one.

time out for you: Give yourself a break and retreat to your bedroom or somewhere quiet and read a book or a magazine for a few minutes. Remember life happens. Rather than keep track of your mistakes, learn something from your experience and all that follows – then you can stop feeling guilty and move on to the next good thing.

don't agree on discipline

You both want your kids to be well behaved, but you just can't agree on how to make it happen.

When it comes to choosing our partner, we tend to choose our diametric opposite in terms of personality. So if we are vivacious, outgoing and social, we tend to be attracted to a quiet, sensitive, ordered sort of person. If we are impatient, goal-focused and fiery, odds are our beloved will be calm, gentle and inclined to 'go slow' under pressure.

When we think of our own upbringing and reflect on how we wish to parent in particular situations, generally we make two lists: the positive things our parents did which we would want to emulate in our own parenting; and the things we promised we would never do or say to our own children (yet under stress, to our alarm and horror, we hear our parents' exact words coming out of our mouths!).

Sometimes the parenting advice we read about or receive from others may be contradictory. It's no wonder then that it seems impossible to decide what to do in some of those particularly trying parenting moments!

Given these three factors – opposite temperaments, different upbringings and loads of conflicting advice – the real miracle is that we find any area of agreement when it comes to raising our children. So let's not be surprised that we find ourselves disagreeing over whether bedtime should be at 7 p.m. or 8 p.m.; whether they should use fingers or cutlery when eating; or whether electronics are educational or just entertaining.

I'm a great believer in writing things down. Unless we are able to write down a description of the problem, it is unlikely we have enough clear information to resolve our differences.

write down:

- your wants, your partner's wants;
- your partner's perspective from the point of personality and upbringing;
- your perspective from the point of personality and upbringing.

the issue:

I want the children in bed by 6.30 p.m. because by

that time I am exhausted and so are the children. My husband wants 'quality time' with them when he gets home from work but it means we don't start cooking our dinner until at least 8 p.m.

His personality – My partner has lots of energy and loves to play, especially with the children.

My personality – I need things to be relatively ordered. I get very tired and need down-time and personal space.

His upbringing – His father travelled a lot and always came home late and tired. He doesn't want to be that sort of a Dad.

My upbringing – We always had to be in bed by the time Dad got home. He would come and sit on our bed for a chat and a story and turn off our lights.

In this scenario, no wonder Mum and Dad disagree!

Some people are born with calm strategies but for the majority of us, we have to work at it - especially when it comes to parenting.

Don't fight infront of
your children.

Often by the time you have got as far through the issue as writing it down, you are already able to see it is not about the 'right way' or 'wrong way', but about two understandable different positions. This way of analysing the problem may enable you to sit down together, describe both positions and begin to work out 'Our Way' for your unique combination as a parent-couple.

avoid discussion traps

There are many psychologists and couple therapists who talk about fighting fair and staying 'grown-up' instead of having a childish ('You never . . .', 'Well, you always . . .') spat. Here is advice from two people's books that I have found useful for keeping me out of a useless row.

Stephen Karpman talks about three positions in his Karpman's triangle we can avoid:

- The Persecutor – when we berate and browbeat and point out as many faults as we can.
- The Victim – where we whine, complain and nag.
- The Rescuer – where we rush to defend someone who may be entirely capable of looking after their own interests or coping with a small frustration at that moment. (I include children here. Sometimes they can manage without an ice block or the tenth swing without their world collapsing.)

Eric Berne, the father of Transactional Analysis, was the person who first spoke about our responding from our Parent, Adult and Child ego states. He recommends we avoid a Child state during an argument where we blurt out – loudly and often nastily – all the resentments we have built up which may have nothing to do with the issue at stake, or where we drop into a temper tantrum of our own. He also suggests we keep out of the Critical Parent state whereby we criticise, point out faults and lecture on reforming our partner's wicked ways.

avoid arguing in front of your children

Children rely on us setting boundaries around their behaviour to give them a sense of security and safety. When we argue in front of them or within earshot, we destroy that safety and negatively model yelling and arguing as a means of getting one's own way.

Provided there is no immediate need to protect your child from harm, you are far better off saying, 'Do what your Dad – or Mum – says now,' even if you disagree with what your partner has requested. Usually it is more important for your child to see you pulling together than to have some childish refusal or request met immediately. When you use the power of two, you will be amazed how fast your child can get over it.

You can easily go over the situation together later once your child is asleep to look at what each of you was trying to achieve and why, and to find a solution that is good for your child and that you can both live with.

different households

In an ideal world, we would all agree on the rules and apply them across all establishments. However, very few of us live in this ideal world and it is a comfort to know toddlers and young children are easily capable of following different rules in different places.

Where parents are separated, it would be lovely to think that for the sake of the child they could agree about the boundaries of child behaviour. In the real world, it might come as a nice surprise to you to know that your child will rapidly learn the rules of each household. It is easier and more likely to work if you focus on what the rules will be under your own roof, and to make any child handover with your ex-partner as swift and amiable as possible. Expect your child to be a bit disrupted for a few hours when they return back home before happily settling back into the rules of your household.

So next time you and your partner are in disagreement about a parenting issue, remember to pull together in front of your child, try to understand both points of view and find a solution you both can live with.

Diane Levy, Family Therapist

do you have a favourite?

Think about your family of origin. Were any of your siblings perceived as Mum or Dad's favourite? Was any grandchild perceived as more special than the others?

I am sure if you challenged your parents, or your grandparents, they would be horrified at the suggestion and strongly declare, 'I love all my children/ grandchildren equally.'

How about your own children? You probably love them all equally, but do you like them all equally? Do you understand them all equally?

Many of us get ourselves tied in knots trying to make everything absolutely fair and equal so we can never be accused of favouring one child over another. Our job, as parents, is to meet our children's needs and help them develop their talents as best as we possibly can.

But once we have got over the hang-up that we must do everything absolutely equally with each of our children, we then free ourselves up to enjoy the differences in our children and meeting their needs according to age, temperament and inclinations.

gender favourites

The 'favourite' is often perceived to be a particular gender in a particular generation. For

example, how often have we heard the saying 'Daddy's Girl'? The implication is that just because the child is a girl, she is more likely to be favoured by Dad. (Unfortunately, 'Mummy's Boy' has an altogether different connotation and belies the special relationship that exists between mothers and their sons.)

Alternately, we may line up the gender war as 'gender favouring gender' as in all the girls (Mum included) are ganging up on poor Dad. The reality is there is natural warmth of understanding and commonality between parent and child of the same gender, and a natural magnetism between parent and child of opposite gender.

generational favourites

Often one grandchild finds particular favour because, 'She is the first girl in three generations.'

Favouritism - is it really okay? You probably love all your children equally, but do you like them all equally? Do you understand them all equally?

> There are some children we find easier to get on with and some with whom finding harmony is trickier.

or because 'He is a true... (insert whichever family surname has relevance!)' Children are very quick to pick up when a beloved grandparent seems to favour a characteristic that only one grandchild has and, not surprisingly, they become both bewildered and hurt. If we find ourselves in this situation, what can we do?

Any attempt to instruct grandparents to behave in a fairer way is likely to send them into a frenzy of denial. A gentler approach of, 'Sam finds it really upsetting when he hears you saying how wonderful it is to have the first granddaughter in three generations. He feels like he's not as important to you,' may alert a sensitive grandparent to the effect they are having.

What if you come up against a blank wall? Our natural impulse when our child tells us about favouritism is to try to protect them and say something like, 'Oh I'm sure Grandma loves you all equally.' In fact, if the favouritism is obvious and unchangeable, we are better off acknowledging our children's accurate observation and supporting their feelings about it: 'I'm sorry that Grandma does that. It really isn't fair. You're right to be upset.' Then our child feels heard and supported by us.

personality types

It is likely that although we love all our children equally and do our best to meet all their needs, we may inadvertently find some personality types more attractive, or more irritating, than others. For simplicity, I am going to use four personality descriptions:

- **The Controller** – who likes everything done their way and gets angry when things don't go their way.
- **The Charmer** – who loves fun and company, and is generally positive if somewhat noisy.
- **The Perfectionist** – who likes things to happen in a precise and predictable way.
- **The Peace-lover** - who hates rows and confrontation and

tries to avoid doing things they don't want to do.

When it comes to choosing our partners, we often choose our opposites: The Controller and the Peace-lover are attracted to each other, as are the Charmer and the Perfectionist. However, we cannot pick our children's personalities - we get what we are given!

family favourites

Often, as parents, we find the personality we chose in our partner very attractive when it shows up in our child.

When our child is just like us, we find that child very familiar in the way in which they operate and thus easier to understand. The opposite may also be true... the characteristics we don't like in ourselves may profoundly irritate us when we see them in our child.

When our child is unlike either parent, we might find them rather difficult to read. Look around extended family or friends and see who is similar to your 'unfamiliar' child. Pick someone you really like. They will usually be able to help interpret your child's behaviour and to help you to understand what motivates your child to behave badly or well.

So to sum up, let's stop frantically denying there are differences in the way we relate to our children, and accept there are some children we find easier to get on with and some with whom finding harmony is trickier.

Having acknowledged that and understood our responses a little better, we can make sure we are being fair, not playing favourites, and just loving our children for who they are.

**Diane Levy,
Family
Therapist**

discipline disagreement

Q: My partner and I have a blended family. We have a 22-month-old together and we each have a daughter from previous marriages – I have a three-and-a-half-year-old and he has an 11-year-old. The problem in our relationship is discipline. We just can't agree on how to do it. I know I have been inconsistent in my parenting, and despite wanting to change, I never follow through. The problem is I don't know what is appropriate discipline? I have tried 'Time Out', scooping up and into the room advice, but nothing seems to work. I have been following the 'Time Out' in the room strategy for months on end but there is still no change and my three-and-a-half-year-old really pushes the boundaries. She does, however, listen to my partner because she knows she can't get away with it. My partner is getting tired of her naughty behaviour but we don't agree on the right discipline method as he wants to 'consistently smack.' I would like some 'real' advice as to what to do.

A: Although we have all been assured that parents will not be acting outside the law if we lightly smack our children, none of us would want to be the cases where this is tested out in a Court of Law. In any case, by the term 'consistently smacking', I infer that your partner would like you to use smacking in a repeated way and I do not think that is the best or the wisest way to teach a child to behave – and probably not in the spirit of the Law. Your best way of getting your partner to give up on the idea of smacking your daughter is to come up with an effective and consistent way of getting your daughter to do as you tell her. You are trying to use 'Time Out' as a punishment when she doesn't do as she is told and your partner thinks that smacking would be a more effective punishment. I would like to persuade you both to give up on the idea of punishment because that usually raises the resistance of a child and causes resentment. Instead think in terms of making it clear to your daughter that once you have asked her to do something, nothing else is happening until that is done. ASK her once. Move over to her and TELL her firmly what you expect. If she does not comply, you need to ACT. Put her in her room until she is ready to do as told. You said you have trouble with following through. If you are adopting the non-punishment option, all you have to do is wait until your daughter changes her mind. If you stop trying to persuade, plead or threaten, there really is nothing to do but get on with your day until she is ready to co-operate. Then she may leave her room. If you start with the first fuss of the morning, for example, getting dressed and tell her she cannot leave her room until she is prepared to hold still while you dress her, you will establish yourself as boss for the morning. Make sure the first three requests of the morning happen and the rest of the day will go a lot sweeter. Your partner clearly wants to support you in your parenting. The best thing he can do, if he notices you are struggling, is to stand shoulder-to-shoulder with you and say to your daughter, 'You need to do what your Mum has asked.' This way you two are a team and neither of you have to struggle with the idea that his parenting is different from yours.

Diane Levy

tired and grumpy

Q: I sometimes get very tired and end up getting grumpy with my children and then regret it. What can I do to turn this into a much nicer situation for all of us?

A: Parenting is very demanding work so it is not surprising that we find ourselves getting grumpy and then yelling and nagging. Unless there are other contributing factors, what usually makes us tired and grumpy is the nagging that we have to do to get our children to do as they are told. I have found that, if I find myself in a continuously grumpy state, I try awfully hard to be nice to my children. They often misunderstand my niceness as permission to behave badly. Then I wind up twice as angry and then feel mad at myself for that. Instead of trying to make up for it by being nice when you are tired, we are better off sticking to our normal house rules.

Diane Levy

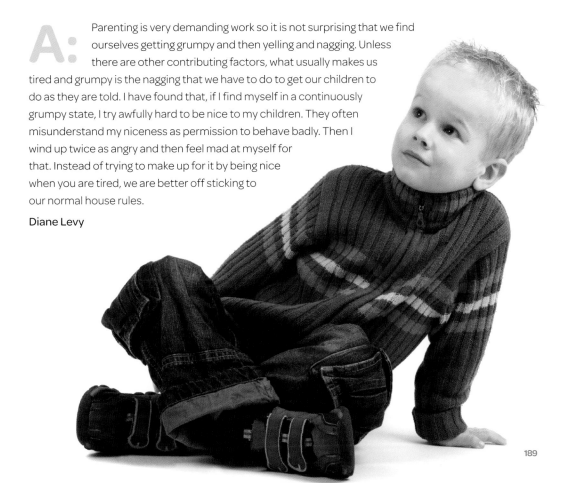

feeding.

feeding milestones

Ever heard the saying that a 'good eating' child is a reflection of a good parent while a 'poor eating' child demonstrates a parental short-coming?

Well, it's simply NOT true! Whether your child is a good eater or a fussy eater, it is all a normal part of their eating skill development.

The following is a guide of how children develop their eating skills in the early years. It is intended as a general guide only as every child develops individually at their own pace.

age 2–3 years

At this age children tend to spill a lot of food while eating. They can place a spoon into their mouth, hold a cup and chew most foods (but are still prone to choking on some foods so always supervise). Some children may begin to 'dawdle' at meal times, often demanding to feed themselves and displaying strong likes and dislikes of certain foods.

If your child wants the same food every day and dislikes other foods, the trick is not to make a big fuss about it – eventually he will move on to a 'new' favourite food. Keep offering other healthy choices with his favourite food rather than the favourite food on its own. For example, offer him his favourite jam sandwich as well as a piece of fruit and a dairy product. By offering only his favourite

food, he will simply demand 'another' favourite food if he is still hungry.

Meal time dawdlers can be infuriating – but try to be patient! Children need time to learn about their eating environment and will often touch and explore their food before actually tasting and eating it. Allow them a reasonable amount of time (20–30 minutes) then simply remove the food without fuss.

age 3–4 years

Around this age, children can chew most foods without choking. They can hold the handle of a cup, use a fork and are likely to begin requesting their favourite foods and show more of an interest in food. Their choices will also be influenced by things they are learning and other factors around them such as colours, shapes, letters and products being advertised on television and in print media.

A great way to encourage children to eat food that doesn't appeal to them is to use biscuit cutters to create food into different shapes. Let your children get involved in the preparation of food to help foster an ongoing interest in food and to show them it can be interesting and fun – let them put toppings on a pizza, create different shaped biscuits or sandwiches using biscuit cutters, ice their biscuit creations, pour coloured water from one container to another, etc.

age 4–5 years

Children are good at self feeding by this age and can use a knife and fork. With their growing vocabulary, they also tend to talk more during meal times rather than eat. They become more

' Children need time to learn about their eating environment and will often touch and explore their food before actually tasting and eating it. '

influenced by what their peers are eating at kindy or childcare, and are keen to know where food comes from, how it is made, etc.

During this stage of development, the battle of the vegetables (and getting children to eat them) can begin. It has been suggested that infants should be introduced to vegetables before fruit as this could prevent a preference for the sweeter, milder taste of fruit. However, if your child still refuses vegetables, let them get involved by selecting the vegetables when you're out shopping; or grow your own vegetable garden together and let them choose what vegetables they want to grow.

Schedule meals and snacks at intervals when your child is more likely to feel hungry (but not too hungry), then include a small amount of the 'offending' food with other small amounts of favourite foods.

Remember, rigid and controlling approaches to how your child eats could impair the development of their eating skills. Instead encourage them by talking about food and let them discover, in their own time, so they eventually learn to acknowledge their internal cues for hunger and fullness.

Nikki Hart, Nutritionist

breakfast battles

Q: I believe in a good breakfast to start our day and would like to teach this to our daughters. I don't have any problems with my nine month old as she likes her breakfast – and I still spoon-feed her. The problem is our two and a half year old. Most days I have to help by spoon-feeding her cereal so she can finish her bowl. Before I had our second child, I was working full-time and because I had to leave home early, I would spoon-feed my eldest to speed things up. When our second child was big enough to sit in the highchair next to her, our oldest showed off that she could feed herself. But this didn't last long. These days I have to spoon-feed both of them to get breakfast down. I have tried bribes, threats, and keeping her in the highchair until she has finished her bowl. Today she sat in her highchair for two hours. Am I being unreasonable? She is a clever girl with very good language skills and I have tried to give her reasons, which I am sure she understands, but still have no luck.

A: I am not sure from your letter, but I am going to assume your daughter is willing to feed herself quite well at most other meals but is only resistant at breakfast. Firstly, you need to establish when she naturally gets hungry in the morning. During the weekend, don't offer any food at all and wait until she gets naturally hungry and asks for food. Then you will have some idea of whether part of the problem is that she simply isn't hungry early in the morning. Many children are not hungry early in the morning, generally at a time when we need them to have breakfast before we leave home. Since feeding herself requires an effort that is not motivated by hunger, she would rather be fed or go without. It simply isn't worth the fight, the damage to your relationship with your daughter or starting the day with such disharmony. Feed her – and try to enjoy the process if possible – and at least you will know that she goes off on her adventures for the day with a reasonable breakfast inside her, having had a pleasant time with her Mum. An alternative is to give her a liquidised breakfast that she may more readily (and enjoyably for you) drink by herself.

Diane Levy

fussy eater

Q: I have problems feeding my three year old who is a really fussy eater. I have tried everything to get her interested in food and to eat a varied diet, but am getting nowhere. She won't try any new foods even though I have tried repeated exposures. She loves cooking with me but refuses to try anything unless it is chocolate cake or pikelets. I serve her small portions at mealtimes and try to be relaxed saying it's fine if she doesn't want to eat anything (although deep down it tears me apart). At the table she will tell me she doesn't like anything on her plate. I generally try to ignore this but often she goes to bed without any dinner. She is never hungry at breakfast and isn't keen to eat until mid-morning. I don't let her fill up on fluids before mealtimes. I also have a one year old who is, so far, a good eater and my three year old is only too happy to feed her all manner of foods but refuses to try any herself. She is a healthy, bright and intelligent child and her physical development seems to be on track. I really don't know where to go from here. Should I just give in and let her eat what she wants?

A: The thing to be reassured by is that your little girl is healthy and doing well with regards to physical development, so she is obviously not starving or malnourished! By the age of three, your child wants to control her environment and can request favourite foods and will have an interest in food (that is why she is happy to feed her younger sister). So it's not a matter of 'giving-in' to what she wants to eat; rather it's about using my favourite tactic – the 'One Bite Rule'. This works by presenting a meal that will include a small serve of the food your child insists she doesn't like. The rule is – 'you must have one bite. If you don't, then you must leave the table immediately without having any of the other "favourite foods" and go to bed (missing out on family time and story)'. The child may weep, groan and even gag, but they rarely choose to go to bed over just ONE bite – children simply won't starve themselves! The one-bite rule appeals to me because it allows you to be firm and to discover what your child really doesn't like or is simply too scared to try. Be aware that for many children the term 'healthy' has a negative meaning. Being 'healthy' can be perceived as not being allowed to eat favourite foods, so using this angle at meal times can be detrimental to trying new foods.

Nikki Hart

only eats what he wants to eat

Q: My son is 22 months old and has always been very independent especially when it comes to food. He'll try everything once but will only eat what he wants to eat. The main problem is that when he is served anything that resembles dinner food, he takes a couple of bites and then says, 'Out!' I get him out of his highchair only after some gentle coercing to eat a bit more and he knows that if he wants anything else to eat before the next day, it will be his dinner or nothing. Because he doesn't like non-sweet food, he starves. He used to eat and enjoy a variety of food – chicken, fish, red meat, vegetables, eggs, rice, crackers, etc., but has become more stubborn since weaning and now refuses the lot. I have tried changing dinner to lunch time, creating 'food pictures', gentle encouragement, and more, but nothing seems to work. I don't want to force him to eat and or make a fuss where food is concerned, but the fact he eats nothing from 1 p.m. until the next morning, makes me worry he's not getting enough nutrients. Am I doing the right things or is he an exceptional case where I should break the rules?

A: While this sounds crazy, almost all children, if left to their own devices when it comes to food, will get all the nutrients they need within about 10 per cent. Children are able to determine when they are full and what they need most. It is we as parents who disturb their natural appetite. As long as you keep encouraging variety and introducing these once liked but now rejected foods over and over again, he will eventually expand his food repertoire. It can take up to 10 exposures for a child to finally accept a food. Maybe you need to 'bore' him with repetition – by this I mean expose him for 10 times to one rejected food at a time – rather than giving in to trying to please with different rejected foods each day. As long as his growth is good in both length and weight, you are not doing him any harm.

Nikki Hart

doesn't eat vegetables

Q: Our four year old hasn't eaten vegetables, other than potatoes and sometimes peas and baked beans, since he was 18 months old. He eats selected fruit (bananas, oranges, apples, watermelon), meat (meat chips, chicken nuggets), toast and bread. But the list of what he won't eat is much longer. His fussiness is frustrating, yet we religiously dish him up vegetables every day. He can also get into the fridge easily and often helps himself to apples, sometimes eating up to six a day. We try not to give him unhealthy things but he's been without a wide range of food for so long.

A: Fussy eating by a child can drive a parent crazy. Cooking can intensify smell and taste so if cooked vegetables are being regularly rejected by the child, try serving a plate of raw or blanched vegetables (raw beans, carrot and courgette sticks or blanched cauliflower florets) with a vegetable dip such as guacamole. For children aged five years or older, a small bowl of frozen peas makes a fun snack. I'm not convinced your child has an eating disorder – rather he sounds like just a very plain eater. My concern is his easy access to food he likes, such as the apples in the fridge. By filling himself up on this food it means he's less likely to try other foods at meal times. I would restrict his access to the fridge and encourage him to try at least one bite of anything he doesn't like on his plate. This can help you discover what your child really doesn't like or is simply too scared to try. If after this you still feel your son has an eating disorder, I suggest asking your doctor for a referral to a registered dietitian.

Nikki Hart

helps herself to food

Q: I have a problem with my four year old who helps herself to food all of the time. We have tried locks on the fridge and cupboards but she breaks them, and we really feel she needs to learn she simply can't go helping herself whenever she pleases. She knows she is always given three meals a day plus morning and afternoon tea, and if she is hungry any time in between, she may ask for a snack or drink. But instead she helps herself to food, even when I am in the kitchen. We praise her when she does ask, and when she doesn't and is caught (usually four or five times a day), she is told it is not acceptable and sent to her room. She is a lovely and helpful girl when she is by herself, but can be particularly defiant when her siblings are around.

A: If I could interview any of your children and ask them if they are allowed into the fridge and cupboards to help themselves, I am sure they would all confidently answer, 'No.' With five eating opportunities being offered each day, plus being able to ask if they want (it is unlikely that they will need) an extra snack, going into forbidden places is nothing to do with hunger and everything to do with non-compliance. I am not surprised you mention the locks being broken as I am so often told by parents how their children can manage to get around many safety systems. I carry this vision of the safety lock being put up, the child seeing it as a new and interesting problem to be solved, and the parent waiting and watching the child demolishing it. Make your life simple. Install the locks once more and teach them to be regarded not so much as a fail-safe lock but rather as symbolic. Your children know what they are for, and any attempt to touch them or fiddle with them should result in a swift scoop to their room and a strong reminder, 'You know you are not allowed to go into there.' Skip the praise for asking. If it was going to work, it would have worked by now.

Diane Levy

loves food and eats all the time

Q: How do I stop my daughter from wanting to eat all the time? She has two breakfasts, one by herself and one with Dad. She eats morning tea, lunch, afternoon tea and dinner. The problem is that every time I go into the kitchen, she follows me asking for something to eat. When I am hungry between meals, I resort to hiding in the pantry to quickly snack on something so she doesn't see me and cause a fuss. I have barely cleaned the kitchen bench and loaded the dishwasher when I have to start bringing out food again. She has a healthy diet and thankfully is very slim and energetic so obviously she is burning up a lot of energy. But I feel her need for food is more of an attention thing and wanting something to do rather than hunger?

A: I certainly giggled at the thought of you hiding in your own pantry for a snack! A three year old has high-energy needs but sometimes by eating a 'healthy' diet, a child doesn't always get the calories they need and will feel hungry often. Is she getting enough fat? I know this sounds a strange question coming from a dietitian but small children still need at least a third of their diet coming from fat, such as for example, avocado and cheese, which also provide energy for growing bodies. Our quest for good health sometimes limits the energy a child needs because we have other family members to consider. If, however, you think she is getting enough fat and it isn't hunger making her request more food, try looking at her fibre intake. A little more fibre might help to keep her feeling full so she is not demanding food so frequently. However, be careful if she is slim and active as you don't want her losing weight by not achieving enough calories for growth. Higher fibre alternatives include Weetbix rather than low-fibre cereals such as rice bubbles or cornflakes, soft wholemeal bread in place of white varieties, and baked beans instead of spaghetti. Since she isn't an overweight child and is 'bright and busy', she may just be hungry because of her activity levels. If you are still worried, check her growth with your Plunket nurse or contact a NZ registered dietitian for individualised nutrition advice.

Nikki Hart

snack ideas for 2-5 year olds

Just as a race car needs lots of regular pit stops to keep in the race, so, too, do little people on the go. If children go without food too long, their blood sugar and energy levels may drop and they're likely to become tired and grumpy.

Young children have small tummies and they need to eat little and often. Their fast metabolisms burn food quickly so snacks are important to keep the fuel tank from running on empty. But it's not always easy to persuade little ones to eat healthy snacks - especially when you've run high and dry of interesting and creative ideas.

Three meals and at least two snacks will be needed each day. Serving your child a nutritious snack, mid-morning and mid-afternoon, can help ward off any potential grizzles and provide him with enough fuel to get through the day; and the more active he is, the more energy he needs from food. Snacks need only be small, just enough to keep him

satisfied until the next meal, but shouldn't take the place of a meal.

Stick to foods that are low in fat, salt and sugar (important for young developing teeth to remain cavity free), such as vegetable sticks, fruit, sandwiches, bread rolls, crackers, muffins, fruit bread, fruit buns, cereals, popcorn, yoghurt, cheese, etc.

fun and nutritious

Just as importantly presentation which can make the difference between whether or not your child will try it, let alone eat it, especially for less exciting foods. Try cutting food into fun shapes – use biscuit cutters for sandwiches or a knife to cut food into squares, circles and triangles. Make fruit kebabs using straws with sliced banana, kiwifruit, pineapple and orange pieces. Chop up carrots and celery sticks and provide small 'dipping' bowls of hummus, cream cheese, etc. Roll a cheese wedge in a slice of ham.

Serving snack foods in bright-coloured containers of different shapes and sizes may also encourage consumption – little fingers love to open and close small objects, and it's excellent for fine motor development too!

out and about snacks

If you're heading out with your littlie, especially during snack periods, take a small lunchbox of finger foods for munching on, such as a mini sandwich, piece of fruit, cheese and crackers (and pop a travel pack of wipes in your bag for the clean up after!).

what to drink

Children need at least one litre of fluid each day so offer a drink at each snacktime. Water is best. Milk is also a great drink; serve after or between meals, and limit consumption to no more than 500ml per day. More milk than this can fill up little tummies so they are too full to eat foods containing other nutrients they need. Juice (if served) should be very dilute, no more than five parts water to one part juice (some health professionals recommend 1:10 as even naturally occurring sugars can cause tooth decay), and provided only once a day. A good way to ensure this dilution is to nearly fill a glass or jug with water and use the juice to colour it slightly.

offer variety

To stay healthy and grow, it's important young children eat a variety of different foods. Snack foods should be chosen from the different food groups, and should be nutritious, and low in fat, salt and sugar. Save food and drinks high in sugar, fat and salt for special treats .

When other children come to play serve a platter of different snacks to pick and choose from - cheese cubes, crackers, apple slices, orange wedges, banana pieces, and sandwich shapes. Works a treat and something for everyone.

On the following two pages we have compiled, with the help of experts, healthy and easy-to-eat snack ideas for 2-5-year-olds that you can also include in lunch boxes.

snack ideas for 2-5-year-olds

grapes
(seeded & halved)

pita bread & hummus

blueberries

pikelets

pineapple

scone

cucumber

raisin bread

strawberries

Teach littlies to s
down while eatir
snacks too.

Cut foods into sm
easily chewed fin
foods for littlies

raisins & sultanas

celery

yoghurt

sliced meat

corn thin

cooked pasta

dried apricots

Go for a variety of
foods from day to day
and week to week.

Three meals and at
least two snacks will be
needed each day.

weetbix with spread

pear

peaches

creamed rice

beetroot

cooked carrot

mini muffin

always supervise feeding - some foods may cause choking in younger children.

rice crackers | cheese | raspberries | mini sandwiches | peas

kiwifruit | crumpets | mousetraps | banana | mandarins & oranges

plain biscuits | cherry tomatoes | boiled egg | Children need at least 1 litre of fluid each day. Limit milk consumption to no more than 500ml per day. | plain popcorn

mini corn cobs | Rub peeled apple with a few drops of lemon to prevent browning. As well as fresh, you can also use canned or stewed fruit. | apple | crispbread with spread | watermelon

plums | corn fritters | dried cranberries | avocado | crackers

index